Faith

What Is It?

ISBN-13: 978-1-950252-02-2

Faith

What is It?

By Summer McClellan

To *Carol* and *Walter Kidd*

Whose faith has helped me through many trials.

Other Books

by Summer McClellan

The Impossible Marriage

Grace What is It?

Passing the Tests of Life

Broken Hearts

Dreams A Window to the Unseen

Love What is It?

What Can I Do for God

Satan Has No Power Over You

Light and Darkness

Hope What is It?

Jesus is Our Example

Foreword

One day my phone rang. It was my mom. She had just gotten back from a wonderful revival meeting at her church and was bursting with excitement to tell me an awesome revelation that was shared at the meeting. She built it up so much; I braced myself for some deep, inspiring message.

"The new wine is in the cluster of the grapes," she said it slowly and emphatically with excitement in her voice. "The new wine is in the cluster of the grapes?" I repeated. I don't know what I was expecting but I had no idea what that meant.

She repeated it a few more times. It obviously was ripe with meaning, but I didn't get it. I don't remember how the conversation ended, but I puzzled over her deep revelation for a while, until it started to make sense to me too.

My own paraphrase goes something like this. All of us carry a part of God, our own little revelation, a gift, ministry or perspective, a piece of God known only to us through our gifting and experiences. A part that the rest of the body needs. Also, a part that is only released when we are crushed and willing to be humble, to lose our identity and take on Christ Jesus's.

I think that's what makes my sister's books so special, this one and also the first one, *The Impossible Marriage*, is that it is written from a crushed grape pouring her new wine out for others benefit. A sweet drop of new wine, crushed in the wine press of life, but full of revelation and insight about the God she has diligently served throughout the years.

If you would like to see Him a little clearer and know Him a little better, then read on and be blessed.

Carol Kidd

Introduction

Faith was a grey area to me. As a new Christian and a young girl, I wanted faith, but I wasn't quite sure what faith was. I heard that with faith I would be able to move mountains and to ask whatever I wanted, and it would be done for me.

I wanted my eyes healed. I am nearsighted and I had been wearing glasses since I was in third grade, thick glasses. I didn't want to wear thick ugly glasses anymore. I had asked my parents for contact lenses, but my dad had said no because they were much too expensive.

I used to pray for my eyes to be healed. I would shut myself away and pray and pray and try to conjure up enough faith for my eyes to be healed. I would sit there with my eyes closed for hours praying. Then I would peek my eyes open to check and see if I could see without my glasses. Were my eyes healed? They weren't. I had gotten other prayers answered before; I must have had some faith. I would pray and work myself into a Pentecostal frenzy trying to get my eyes healed but it didn't work.

I finally got a little older, got a job and saved up enough money to buy my own contact lenses. I still wanted my eyes healed though; I hated sticking those things in my eyes.

One morning I woke up and I could see. I blinked in

amazement. Yes, I could see! I ran down the stairs screaming, "I can see, I can see! I'm healed I'm healed!" My mother and sister were in the kitchen getting breakfast. "I am healed, my eyes are healed!" I shouted to them again. I couldn't believe it, finally, after praying for years, God had healed my eyes. My mother and sister were standing there staring at me, dumbfounded, their mouths dropped open in amazement.

Suddenly I realized my contacts were in my eyes. The reason I could see was that I had forgotten to take my contacts out the night before. I had slept in them all night! I was so disappointed. Didn't I have enough faith? What is faith? I needed to know. The Bible says without faith it is impossible to please God. I need to know this.

Many years have passed since then. This book is about what I have learned about faith and just what faith is. Please read on.

Contents

Volume Four   Principles of Faith

Volume Five   The Hall of Faith

Volume One

Summer's Story

Chapter One

Growing Faith

For by grace, you have been saved through faith, and that not of yourselves; it is the gift of God, not of works, lest anyone should boast. Ephesians 2:8-9

The Bible tells us we are saved by faith. We are born into God's kingdom, by faith. It is our beginning in this new life, this life where our spirits are born again. We receive eternal life through Jesus Christ. The Bible even tells us that this faith is a gift of God. God gives us faith to be saved.

It also tells us in scripture that God gives each of us a measure of faith. *For I say through the grace given to me, to every man that is among you, not to think of himself more highly than he ought to think; but to think soberly, according as God has dealt to every man the measure of faith. Romans 12:3* God starts us all off with a measure of faith. It is up to us to grow in faith.

When we first get saved and come into God's kingdom, we are new to the things of God and new to things of faith. We are spiritual babies. No matter what age we are when we come to the Lord, we are babies in the spirit. As we begin to take our first tottering steps of faith, our proud Father is delighted, and it seems every prayer is answered. But after a time, our Father expects us to mature and grow and exercise our faith. Just like we exercise and strengthen a muscle we need to exercise our faith. Now our Father stands back and expects us to walk on our own. I don't mean He leaves us. He never leaves us. I mean He expects us to now use our faith and receive the answers to our prayers.

I was fourteen when I became a Christian. In my baby phase I made a huge request of God with my new faith. I wanted to go to the Holy land, so did my twin sister, Carol. We had gone to a Gospel concert shortly after we got saved. It was the Blackwood Brothers, a gospel quartet. They were taking a tour of people to the Holy land and talked about it at the concert. This was fall and the tour was in January. I prayed about it. We came home and told our parents about it and of course it was out of the question. My parents were not rich and how many people let their fourteen-year-old kids travel around the globe without them.

Well, some unexpected things happened. My dad had been saving up his money to give my sister and I a year in private school. Instead, he got a job in a new town several hours away. He had this money set aside for the school, but the new town was small and had no private school. I think my parents may have felt a little guilty because it was a big change to move us to a new town. So suddenly, at the last minute, our parents changed their minds and they decided to let us go on the Holy land tour. Carol and I couldn't believe that we got to go. My parents are still scratching their heads wondering why they let us go off without them; they worried about us the whole time we were gone.

It was a wonderful experience. It was the trip of a lifetime. We were in Jordan and saw Petra; we also saw the cities Jericho and Jerusalem. We saw Golgotha where Jesus was crucified, we saw His tomb. The Bible came alive to us. We also went to Egypt; I have been in the pyramids. It was an amazing experience. As adults neither my sister nor I have been able to travel so having had this trip means even more to us. God was rewarding my first baby steps of faith! I wanted to go to the holy land, and I went!

As time went on it wasn't so easy to get my prayers answered. Sometimes I got my prayers answered and sometimes I didn't. I wasn't a baby anymore; it was time to grow in faith. Sometimes I felt I had faith, and nothing happened, sometimes I had many doubts. I couldn't quite seem to get a grasp of what faith was or how to not have doubts. It was they grey area again. Just what is faith? Is it a confident feeling? I had so much to learn at this point. I just wasn't sure. It was time to grow up spiritually. To learn about just what it is I can get from God.

Have you ever gone shopping with a little child? I just went to the mall with my three-year-old granddaughter, Hailey, yesterday. She was so cute; we went into a store that was all girly things. I was hoping to find some hair clips on the clearance rack. Hailey, knowing nothing about money, wanted everything. She found cute things everywhere. She would wander over to some stuffed animals {her weakness} and pick them up and hug them in delight, then she would holler, "Look at what I found!"

Over and over, she kept finding wonderful things to her little mind. I would pry them out of her arms and tell her we aren't buying toys today. To help herself deal with the devastation that she couldn't buy all this marvelous stuff she would say, "I want that for my birthday!" She said it about a doll, a skirt, many stuffed animals, everything in the toy shop window. It all looked so lovely to her, she wanted everything. We didn't buy anything yesterday, but of course there are things we buy Hailey. I only buy my grandchildren toys at garage sales, and I help her mama get Hailey the things she needs. This summer I had bought her shoes and boots for winter and clothes. There are some things I will buy for her. She is starting to learn that she can't have everything she wants in the store. But when she needs socks and underwear we go and get them. We don't get everything we ask for, but there are things we need to ask for. It is part of growing up. The same is true when we begin to pray. I am still waiting for God to answer my prayer for a million dollars. Yes, I asked Him for a million dollars. I have asked Him for a trip to Hawaii, and many other things.

I was fourteen when I became a Christian; all God heard from me back then was that I wanted a boyfriend. Is it wrong for us to ask for these things? Of course, it isn't. Just like Hailey, we will get some of the things we ask for. There are things we learn as we grow and get to know God better, things that He wants to give us. Things that we know we can have; the answer is yes. We receive those things by faith.

I noticed something, there were some areas that we easier for me to believe God about. For instance, I have always known how God feels about babies. God loves babies and He loves to give babies to married couples. As I got to know God better, I learned how He felt about that.

When Jim and I were newly married, we were going to a home fellowship group. There were quite a few couples going to this fellowship and most of us had children. Jim and I had one at this time also. Three couples in our group did not have children. All three couples were around the age of thirty and had been married for a while. I did some asking around and found out they all wanted children but just had never gotten pregnant.

"I know how God feels about that," I thought to myself, so I prayed for all three of them. I didn't tell them, I did it at home. I didn't pray for a long time; I didn't need to. I knew how God felt about this subject, I knew His heart. He loves babies!!! He loves giving people babies!

I don't think it was any coincidence that after all those years of trying all three of those couples had a baby within that next year. That was an area I understood God about, and I just knew He would give them a baby. Some things were easier to pray about than others. I had an understanding of God in this area, I knew this about Him and how He feels about babies, so I knew God would do it.

Getting to know God better gives us more faith. To know Him is to trust Him. Putting our trust in God in any area of our life moves us into the realm of faith.

One day I had a terrible headache. I have never had a whole lot of faith for healing, but this day I was praying and talking to the Lord, while I had this headache. I asked Him to take it away like I had many other times but never had any results, but this time was different. I asked him to take the headache away and then I thought about how kind and wonderful He is and then I answered the question for Him. "Of course, You will." I answered, suddenly overcome with thoughts of His goodness. Immediately the headache disappeared. Spending time with Him and knowing His nature caused my faith to increase.

We need to grow our faith in God. It is part of growing as a Christian.

Chapter Two

God's Way Not Ours

As a new and praying Christian I was having just a little trouble figuring God out. He just wasn't running things like I thought He should. I felt like I knew what I needed, {everything to be easy}. He was doing everything backwards, what was He thinking?

I guess I had a lot to learn. I just wanted to make it through life without any difficulties and He has eternal goals for me in mind. I remember realizing one day that He was smarter than me and He actually knew what was best. It was an "aha" moment for me when I realized that. Yes, I was a bit dumber than most. I had a very human mindset I wanted God to do things my way, and I would pray very hard for Him to, with no avail. God has a higher purpose for us than we have for ourselves. He is concerned with our eternal outcome. God has our best in mind, and He reserves the right to do what is best for us.

I remember one time when I was fifteen years old. My parents had just bought a house that looked beautiful, my mother's dream house. We lived in beautiful Northern Michigan. The first winter there, the dream house became a nightmare, it had problems. We had trouble with the roof.

We had a huge, beautiful living room with grand, big wooden beams in the ceiling. One day water was pouring out of the beams, in the living room ceiling, like a waterfall. The carpet was soaked. It was all coming from the trouble with the roof.

The roof was covered with a thick layer of ice. My dad after working hard all day would come home and climb a ladder and pound on the ice-covered roof with a hammer trying to knock off the ice. I would be up in my upstairs bedroom and could see my dad outside my window in the freezing cold, pounding on the roof. I would hear him working bang, bang, bang, bang, bang. I couldn't stand it. It was freezing out there and I worried he would fall.

"God," I prayed, "I want You, to knock the ice off the roof for my dad!"

"Do you believe I will do it?" He asked me.

"Yes" I replied, hoping I really did have enough faith.

"If you believe I will do it then I want you to get up at church tomorrow night and tell everyone I will do it."

"Well okay," I said. We hadn't lived in our new town for very long and we didn't know a lot of people. But we had started attending a new church that my sister and I had wanted to go to. It was spirit filled and we bugged our parents to go there, because we wanted to speak in tongues. Our parents weren't thrilled like we were when we went forward for prayer the first time there and we got filled with the spirit and speaking in tongues. They had a little boring church all picked out, but they figured they had better take us to the spirit filled church now, since their daughters were spirit filled.

Tomorrow was the Wednesday night service, and it was less formal than Sundays, they would have a time for people to give testimonies. So, the next night, at church, during testimony time, I raised my hand. I jumped up and told everyone, "Our roof is leaking because it is covered with ice. My dad has to work and work trying to knock the ice off." Then I told them "I have prayed, and God is going to knock the ice off the roof!"

Everyone cheered. Our church believed in miracles. I couldn't wait to get home and see the ice gone. I had it pictured how it would happen, the ice would just come sliding down in one huge sheet, like an avalanche. It would be a miraculous and wonderful event. We pulled into the driveway, and the ice was still on the roof. I wondered if my faith was too small.

Years later I was talking to my sister, and she mentioned the ice on the roof. "I guess I didn't have enough faith," I said, "the ice never slid off the roof."

"Yes, you did!" she exclaimed "Don't you remember what happened?"

I did remember what happened, but I didn't realize until all those years later, until my sister pointed it out to me that God did answer my prayer, just not in the way I was expecting. I was expecting a grandiose ice avalanche to come, powered by God, sliding down in one huge crash. God answered my prayer in a different way.

The next Sunday a man approached my dad at church. "Did the ice come off your roof?" He asked. He had heard my testimony at church Wednesday night.

"No," my dad told him, "It's still there."

"I am an architect," the man told my dad. "I would like to come over and look at your roof."

The architect came over to our house. He looked around. He showed my dad what was wrong with the roof. There was too much insulation, and the roof was getting hot spots. He helped my dad fix the problem. He also recommended a few other repairs my dad did. We never had a problem again with the roof.

Thinking back all these years later I realized God answered my prayer His way, a better way. My way would have been grand, but the ice would have kept forming on the roof every winter. God fixed the problem permanently. My dad also made a lifelong friend. He and the architect are still friends today.

God's ways are so much higher than ours. He will answer our prayers in the way that is best. We may not see it at the time, but we can trust that His ways are the best. Sometimes it takes hindsight and many years and some maturity to realize that God did things in a much better way than we had thought He should.

Many things don't make sense until years later, but one thing I have learned, although things may not make sense at the time, if you give God a situation, like the ice problem on our roof, He will handle it the best way possible, His way.

Chapter Three

Without Faith You Will Die

I was never as happy as when I found out I was pregnant for the first time. In fact, I was giddy. I walked around giggling. I had gotten married in September without any thought of having children whatsoever. I had even started birth control pills. In October my husband and I went to our first marriage seminar. During the seminar the Lord spoke to me about having a baby. It was then I received the revelation from God about how He feels about babies that I mentioned in the last chapter. God told me it was time for me to have a baby and to stop taking birth control. Suddenly I wanted to have a baby, I had no experience taking care of babies, but I wanted one.

I had no period in November and December, and I thought I was pregnant. My periods had never been regular so that was really not uncommon for me, but I worked myself up that I was pregnant. In January my mother got the shock of her life when she found out she was pregnant. She had only my twin sister and I, and we were nineteen. She was definitely not expecting to get pregnant again. Then in January I got a period, and I was devastated. I cried for days, it didn't seem fair, I wanted a baby so bad and my mom was having one.

Then I got invited to my girlfriend's baby shower, I couldn't go, I was to upset. I can't imagine how devastating it must be for women who want a baby and can't have one. After one try, I was a basket case. I was jealous of every woman with a baby.

March came around and I hadn't dared hope I was pregnant again, but I went in for a pregnancy test and it was positive. My due date was November 4. I was so happy. I went to Lamaze classes with my mother; I was her Lamaze coach when her baby, my little sister, was born in August. Seeing my new little sister was wonderful and I couldn't wait to have mine.

I had an especially large baby bump; I was so huge I was sure I would have my baby early, but I didn't. November fourth came and went. I waited and waited and waited until I felt like it wasn't real, I was never going to have a baby. And I kept getting bigger! In fact, I got huge! I couldn't get up by myself. I could barely walk. Finally, on December fifth, I went into labor, a sudden, hard, painful labor. After a very painful day the doctor realized something was wrong and took an X-ray. The baby was in the wrong position and too big. I had to have a C-section. I wanted them to hurry, I wanted out of pain. Finally, they came and put me out.

The next thing I knew was pain, searing pain, worse than anything I had ever felt. Off in the distance I heard moaning, someone was moaning. It was me, moaning. I remember thinking that I was pain, that's what I was. Then I heard a woman's voice say, "You had a boy."

"A boy," my mind tried to comprehend the words. "What is a boy?" I asked myself. Then I realized I was a person, not pain. I was a woman, and I had a baby. I stayed in the hospital eight days and had a long recovery period at home, about six weeks. Of course, it was worth it to have my wonderful little baby boy James Jr. He weighed ten pounds and nine and a half ounces when he was born. He was the second largest baby ever delivered in that hospital.

After a year and a half, I got pregnant again. We had many difficulties during the time I was pregnant. My husband lost his job and only had part time work. I had no money to see a doctor.

We had no money for anything, food was scarce. I decided to try a home birth because I didn't know how we would pay a hospital bill. I prayed about it. God provided a miracle. Near the end of my pregnancy my husband got a full-time job that even offered health insurance.

I went to the new doctor the health insurance provided. He said a home birth was out of the question and sent me to a gynecologist who scheduled another C-section. I had planned to have my tubes tied during the surgery. When it came time to sign the papers for some reason, I just couldn't do it, I couldn't sign.

I had another C-section. This time I had a beautiful

baby girl, Lonna Leigh. And this time I had even more trouble afterwards. Not even just the pain, I didn't feel right. The nurses came to get me up after surgery, but I couldn't get up. If they even lifted the head of the bed, I would immediately pass out. Several days went by and I hadn't even sat up yet. I couldn't, I would black out, and the pain was terrible.

On the third day at about eleven o'clock in the morning I felt better. I instantly felt better. I got up out of bed and I didn't hurt nearly as bad. It was a major turn-around. The nurse came in and said, "You really had us worried." That afternoon I had a visitor from my mother's fiery little Pentecostal church. It was the pastor's wife.

"Our ladies prayer meeting really had prayer for you this morning," the pastor's wife said. I knew by the way she said it something unusual had happened in that prayer meeting. That's why she was there to see me. God had laid me on those ladies' hearts, and they prayed me through. Their prayer meeting was at the same time I started to feel better.

I was right; I had gotten through on these wonderful women's faith. After the pastor's wife left that afternoon, the Lord spoke to me. "Next time you have a baby," He said, "you need to use your faith, or you will die." Within a few minutes God sent confirmation.

The doctor came in to have a talk with me. "Your uterus was as thin as a sheet of paper," he told me. "If you had gone into labor or if you ever go into labor you would die."

Faith, God told me I had to use my faith; there was

the grey area again. I never could quite put my finger on what it was. I wasn't quite sure how to strum up enough of it, but I couldn't have another baby without it. I thought to myself, "I just can't get pregnant again." I had two children to raise now. I didn't want to die.

I wanted to be sure I would never get pregnant again. Birth control pills were out. My Christian doctor said they would destroy an embryo that was already established. So that was out for me. I believe life begins at conception. My husband and I decided to use protection but also decided on a vasectomy to be really safe. It wasn't to be. We just couldn't come up with the money and the one time that we did, a catastrophe that I won't go into now happened the night before it was scheduled, and we couldn't have it done. God was in it. If God says there is going to be another pregnancy, there is. My third child was meant to be. We managed to make it three years before I became pregnant again. I was happy when I found out I was pregnant again but concerned. I didn't want to die. I asked God for help.

"God," I prayed, "I know I don't have enough faith; will You help me to have faith to deliver this baby?"

I had no idea what was coming but I was in for the hardest time of my life!

Chapter Four

The Time of the Ox

Trouble seemed to come from every direction during my third pregnancy. Things were already difficult normally, but they got worse. We lived in Florida in a one-bedroom efficiency apartment, on a second floor. It had no heat and no air. It was full of roaches! We called it the roach hotel. Life was already unpredictable; my husband was an alcoholic and I have never gotten used to it. Every time he drank, I would fall apart. We were always short of funds. If we ran out of gas or the car broke down my husband would have to hitchhike to work until we could scrape up money again. My hands were full with little kids too, I had my two children ages five and three years old and I babysat my mom's two, also aged five and three years old.

Life went from difficult, to a deeper level of difficulty. I started feeling sick; I had morning sickness all day. My husband lost his job and now we had no money. Every day became a challenge. I remember shortly after my husband lost his job the electric bill came in; I couldn't pay it. It seemed impossible. I just didn't know where to get the money. I told the Lord, "If You pay this electric bill, I will believe You for all our bills."

That Wednesday night at church I went to the lady's prayer meeting. One of the ladies started crying and then she stood up and said, "The Lord has showed me that Summer has needs and has done without, even without food. We are going to take up a collection for her." They had never taken up a collection for anyone before and never did again. She passed a hat and collected enough for my electric bill. I was committed to trust God for my bills. My husband started getting a little work here and there.

The good thing about my life was my church. It was a huge church that seated five thousand people. They had services almost every day of the week. Good services, wonderful faith filled meetings, the kind I live for. I would go and go and go. The Lord let me know through strangers that my baby was meant to be. People at church kept coming up to me and prophesying over the baby. One man came up behind me in a morning prayer meeting and spoke, "You are going through a very difficult time," he said, "but this baby was meant to be and God is keeping the baby from the turmoil you are going through." Several similar incidents like this happened.

My husband, Jim, and I began to pray about what to name the baby. The Lord told me plainly to name the baby, Joy. Back then you didn't know if you were having a boy or girl until you had it, but we figured out it was a girl when the Lord gave us the name Joy. Then we started talking about middle names but couldn't decide on anything. Then one night I had a dream. I dreamt I was reading the church bulletin and in the bulletin were the baby announcements. The bulletin said *Jim and Summer McClellan would like to announce the birth of their daughter Joy Belle.* I woke up and thought "That's it! That is her name, Joy Belle."

That morning when Jim woke up, I opened my mouth to tell him the baby's name and before I could speak, he said, "I have decided we're naming the baby Joy Belle." My mouth dropped open in amazement!

"I was just going to say that to you," I told him. We knew something special was happening, but things kept getting harder.

We of course had no health insurance, so I had to see a doctor at the health department. It was a nightmare. They scheduled two appointment times, eight a.m. and noon. If you got the eight-a.m. appointment so did about twenty other girls. You would wait outside the door until the door opened and whoever got in first was the first appointment. I was never quite as pushy as the other girls and usually got pushed to the end of the line. They scheduled everyone the same time, an appointment took hours. We lived in Polk County Florida and there was a county hospital you went to if you had no money. It seemed like something from a third world country. Some of the doctors barely spoke English.

Of course, the whole time I was pregnant I knew I

had to have enough faith this time, like God had told me, or I was going to die. "You have to help me have faith, God" I kept praying, "I am not sure if I have faith or not, I need Your help!"

The baby was due January twenty. As that date approached, if things could get worse, they did. One incident that happened in November was I got a terrible tooth ache. It was my wisdom tooth, and it was rotten. It hurt so bad I couldn't eat. If I bit down on that side of my mouth the pain would about knock me out.

Everyone kept telling me horror stories of people they knew with rotten teeth. Jim told me about a man he had known that had died from a rotten tooth. He wasn't the only one. I was so afraid.

I went to the Health Department again. They had a dentist there a couple of days a week. I went early and waited hours to see him. I finally got in to see him and he told me the tooth was rotten and had to be pulled. Because I was pregnant, he had to have a doctor's note first. I waited all afternoon to see the doctor and get the note but by the time I got the note, the dentist had left. I had been at the health department eight hours. This was on a Wednesday, the next day was Thanksgiving and the dentist wouldn't be back until Monday! "I won't be able to eat until Monday!" I thought.

Wednesday night was lady's prayer at church. I went and got prayer for my tooth. I was so afraid, and I told them about all the people I had heard that died from a rotten tooth. Thank God for the lady's prayer meeting! They dealt with me about the fear. They told me God could handle my rotten tooth, after all God makes teeth and mouths and everything. I repented of the fear and put myself in God's hands.

Something amazing happened, most of the pain left with the fear. I could eat. I ate turkey on Thanksgiving. I went to the dentist on Monday and had my tooth pulled in peace. That was a real lesson to me. Fear makes things bigger than they are and trusting God makes problems smaller. I couldn't believe the difference in the level of pain after I let go of the fear. As I was getting the tooth pulled, I had my mind focused on God and I was at absolute peace.

Troubles kept coming. My husband was out of work again, so he signed up to work out of a union hall. They didn't have enough work for everyone so he got work here and there and he never knew when they would call. His new job was cleaning drag lines. They would usually have him work all night when he worked. One week he worked a couple of days straight and he made four hundred dollars! We were so happy! Then our vehicle, an old dilapidated van broke down, we had to have it fixed. It cost four hundred dollars. We had to pay the mechanic every penny we had. When we went to pick up the van the mechanic told us you need tires. Your tires are so worn there are wires sticking out of them. We had no money for tires.

Not too long after that I had the opportunity to earn some money helping an older lady with errands. I was so thrilled to help Jim earn some money. I made fifteen dollars. I came home excited about it. Jim wasn't home he was out looking for work. He never came home.

I started to worry. I finally got a call from the police station he was in jail. Jim had been in a car accident. Two of our tires blew out at the same time. There were beer cans in the car and Jim was charged with a D.U.I. Jim was given a court date and sent home later that night.

Our car had been impounded and we needed fifty dollars to get it back. With the help of my fifteen dollars, he managed to get fifty dollars together. It seemed every time we got a little money, trouble would swallow it up. There were more problems too. I won't write them all, but one was we were asked to leave our apartment; I thought we were going to be homeless. I spent a lot of time crying. I would bring a pillow into the bathroom and bury my face in it and scream and cry. I didn't want my children to hear me. I wondered if things would ever get better.

I kept going to my wonderful church whenever I could get there. There was always something going on. One morning service I went to regularly. They had a special guest around this time. His mother went to our church, and he was visiting. His name was John Paul Jackson. This was before he was well known. They said he was a prophet.

At this service, I remember thinking to myself, I am going to forget everything and worship God. My troubles hung on me like a weight constantly, but this day I just decided to forget everything. I worshipped God with all my heart. Before the service ended, I had to leave early. Jim had called the church and sent a message in, that he needed the van. The union hall called and needed him right away. I wanted to finish hearing the speaker and I was disappointed. I knew I needed to hear him.

I found out John Paul Jackson was going to be at a home prayer meeting the next night. I got Jim to take me. It was Christmas time now and we went to the most beautiful house I had ever been in. The prayer meeting was at a professional football player's house that went to our church. We were sitting in this beautiful living room with a huge gorgeous Christmas tree and there were a lot of people there.

The prophet John Paul Jackson spoke for a while and then he pointed to me. "Were you the lady that had to leave the prayer meeting yesterday?" he asked.

I nodded.

He began to prophesy to me. He said, "You are in the time of the ox in your life. Everything is heavy.   There have been times when you have been able to pray through situations and everything is all right, but it hasn't been like that this time. You are just trudging through. This baby you are carrying was meant to be." I had heard that many times. Then he continued, "There will be a change of employment coming in 1988 that will bring more finances into your home."

Every one that knew me cheered. This was Christmas time in 1987; I just kept hoping the change of employment was at the beginning of 1988 and not the end. I thought of the prophet's words often, they brought me hope.

January, the month my baby was due, came up and the problems continued. Jim had his court date and went to jail for thirty days. Now I had no income at all, and I missed my husband when I needed him most.

My sister and my dad were scheduled to come and help me after my C-section. I was usually out of commission for weeks after a baby. My sister came at my due date. I went to the County Hospital, but the doctor put off the C-section.

I kept trying to tell him, "My doctor in Michigan told me I can't go into labor! He said it would kill me!"

The county doctor was foreign and barely spoke English. He wasn't going to do it. He ordered stress tests about every five days and just waited.

I kept going to my Wednesday lady's prayer meeting. I sat and sobbed. I told them, "I am supposed to have a C-section and the doctor won't do it! My help is here now, and I won't have anybody when I need them! I am getting kicked out of my apartment and my husband is in jail!!"

They told me God could handle it and that He would send angels to take care of me after the baby was born if He had to. They also said that I should be willing to have the baby any way God chose, even a natural birth, that God could handle anything.

That night I entered a new place, in God. My life was so out of control, and I felt so helpless. I let go of it. I let go of everything. I didn't know what was going to happen, but I couldn't handle any of it anymore. I knew everything was so out of control I could never fix any of it and just decided what ever happened God would just have to deal with it. Every area of my life was a problem. We had two little children already. I didn't have any money, or food, my husband was in jail. I didn't know if we were going to be homeless. My help, my sister and my dad weren't going to be available when I needed them and now, I couldn't get the medical help I needed. I didn't even have gas to get to the stress tests. The county hospital was about thirty minutes away in another town.

I let go. I didn't know what was going to happen next, but I just put everything, every minute, in God's hands. Whatever happened, I just gave it to Him. I was done.

Chapter Five

This Is Faith?

My son had started kindergarten while I was pregnant. One of the other mothers in his class and I became friends. When I had to go to these stress tests every five days, she told me, "I want to do this for you."

She took me to all of them. She even took me to Ponderosa for lunch after one of them. I was in heaven, all the food I could eat, and I was hungry!

I was no longer in control, minute by minute, day by day, whatever happened I had let go. And God had sent this wonderful lady to take me to these tests, and even feed me. I wasn't eating much to save food for my children.

Jim got out of jail at the end of January. On February 8, I went in for another stress test and it showed I was in labor. They admitted me to the hospital. My sister had been in Florida three weeks and had to leave that day. My dad flew in next. On February 9, in the morning the doctor came in and said, "We might as well due the C-section you are already in labor."

The moment of truth had come. I had stopped trying to make things happen, because I had turned everything over to God, and now finally they were doing the C-section.

I told Jim as they wheeled me into the surgery room, "Get a good look at our baby when they bring her out. I don't want them to switch our baby with someone else's."

The hospital was crowded and chaotic, not like the small clean beautiful hospital where we had our first two babies back in Michigan. Jim was posted at the door, outside the surgery room; he was going to get a look at our baby when they brought her through. There was a little window in the door as they wheeled me into surgery; I could see Jim's face looking through the little window. As hard as our marriage was, with Jim's drinking, Jim is like the sunshine to me, when he is near me, I feel warm. We held each other's gaze, through the door, as long as we could. Then they put me out.

The first thing I remember when I woke up was that I wasn't groggy and confused like I normally was after surgery. And most the surprising of all was, I felt no pain! This was totally different. I still was tired and needed rest but there was no pain. I knew somehow, I had passed the faith test, because I was alive, I wasn't groggy, and I had no pain.

Jim was waiting for me. "You should see our baby," he told me, "She has more hair than you do."

Later that day the nurse brought Joy Belle in. She

was bright and alert too, and what a head of hair. We bonded instantly. I knew why the Lord wanted her to be called Joy. I felt such Joy when I held her. We were in the hospital eight days and then we got to go home.

My dad still had a couple of days left of vacation before he had to leave. They all came to get me, in our big old rusty van, my dad, Jim, Jamie our son now six years old and our little girl Lonna three, almost four. By the time we got home I was already done in. Lonna was obsessed with the new baby and kept trying to hold her. I wondered how I would manage things when my dad left. Just the ride home exhausted me. I thought about what the ladies in my prayer meeting told me, that God would send angels to help me if He had to.

God did. He sent me a big black angel. There was an older man that went to our church. He had been an alcoholic and had gotten saved. Now he spent all his time in church and was always filled with the Holy Spirit. He would holler and praise the Lord during church, and then he would dance in the aisles until he got so drunk in the Holy Ghost he would fall on the floor. He was a revival waiting to happen. He was the closest thing to an angel you could get. He stopped to visit Jim the day before my dad left. We called him Brother Gladwin.

I asked Brother Gladwin for prayer. I told him my help was leaving. Jim had started a job and I didn't have the strength to take care of the new baby and my other children. Brother Gladwin got us all in a circle to pray and, boy, did he ever pray. As soon as he was done, I excused myself and fell into bed. I was so exhausted.

The next day I woke up with energy, not my normal amount of energy, more energy than I had ever had before in my life! I felt wonderful. I had more than enough energy to take care of my family. I even taught my six-year son old to ride a two-wheel bike that week. Every day after school I would put the new baby in the stroller and the three-year-old on a tricycle and my six-year-old on his bike and we went to the park. I had never felt so good. It was truly a miracle!

Another miracle happened also; my husband got a new good job. He started at the beginning of March. He made more money than he ever had before. He had that job for seven years.

I thought about all I had been through. I had my baby, and I didn't die. God had told me I had to use faith, or I would die. Not only did I not die, I had no pain, and after Brother Gladwin's prayer I didn't even need a six-week recovery period. I had faith; I passed the test! I was amazed.

I thought to myself, "That was faith?"

I had thought faith was a confident feeling. I thought it was more like I would be so sure that everything was going to be okay that no doubt would be able to come my way. I could never quite put my finger on exactly what faith felt like, because sometimes I seemed to have it, other times I didn't. This was totally different than what I had expected faith would be like. My life had become so out of control, and I felt so powerless, that I had just totally let go. I gave up everything to God. I didn't know what the next minute would bring. I couldn't take anymore, I felt like I was walking blindly forward but I had given everything to God. It was like when I came to the end of myself there was nothing left but God. I had no more plans, attempts or efforts left in me; all my eggs were in God's basket. I had no confidence in myself or my own ability. It definitely was not a confident feeling; it was more like a letting go. I was letting go and letting God. It really wasn't a feeling at all.

So that was faith! That was not at all what I thought faith was!!! I thought it felt confident and strong! This was just the opposite. I felt so helpless I totally let go. I let go of every effort of trying to get done what I thought was supposed to happen and gave it to God.

I want to quote to you something I read years later from my favorite book ever, *The Final Quest*. It summed up what I was learning about faith. We are jumping in the middle of a story, but I want you to hear the part about faith. In this book the author Rick is in a prophetic vision and talking with an eagle. The eagle represents those with a prophetic gifting. They are speaking of a battle Rick had just witnessed, it is a spiritual battle, and those Rick witnessed had gone forward in pride and had been defeated. They speak of Wisdom, who Rick later finds out is Jesus. Focus on what it says about faith.

Since first coming to this mountain, and fighting in the great battle, I now think that most of the right things I did, I did for the wrong reasons, and many of the wrong things I did, I had good motives for. The more I learn the more unsure of myself I feel."

"You must have been with Wisdom a long time,"

the eagle responded.

"He was with me for a long time before I began to recognize Him, but I am afraid that most of that time I was resisting Him. Somehow, I now know that I am still lacking something very important, something that I must have before I go into battle again, but I do not know what it is."

The great eagle's eyes became even more penetrating before he responded, "You also know the voice of Wisdom when He speaks to you in your own heart. You are learning well because you have the mantle. What you are feeling now is true faith."

"Faith?" I shot back. "I am talking about serious doubts!"

"You are wise to doubt yourself. But true faith depends on God, not yourself, and not your faith. You are close to the kind of faith that can move this mountain and move it we must."

These statements on faith stood out to me because I could relate to them. True faith depends on God, not yourself and not your faith. I had asked God to help me when I got pregnant again. I didn't trust my life to my own shaky faith. God did help me. I got to the end of myself and let go. There is one thing we can totally depend on, only one, and that is God. And when we stop trusting everything else and when there is nowhere else to go for help but to God, who is eternally faithful, and we depend on Him, then we have found true faith!

Volume 2

My Sister Carol's Revelations on Faith

Chapter Six

Clothe Yourself with Christ

For as many of you as were baptized into Christ have put on Christ. Galatians 3:27

The phone rang, it was my twin sister, Carol, her voice sounded excited. "Summer," she shouted, "The Lord's been showing me some things."

"Tell me," I replied. I love hearing this kind of stuff.

"Well," she began, "It all started when this picture popped into my mind. I saw myself clothed in Christ. It kind of looked like those blow up sumo wrestler suits people put on, only I was in Jesus."

"Cool" I piped in with a funny picture in my mind of my sister in a giant Jesus suit. I wondered where this was going.

"Our identity is in Christ," Carol continued.

"Remember the verse in the Bible where it says those who are baptized in Christ have put on Christ. Well in the Greek that means we are to put on Christ like clothing."

"Oh" I said, my mind trying to keep up with what she was saying. My sister is a Rhema Bible School graduate and when she studies her Bible, she looks up the meaning in the original language and gets the deeper meaning.

She continued, "Remember when Moses came down from Mt Sinai and they had to cover his face with a veil, because he was so bright with the glory of God, that his face was glowing? Well, it also refers to this in the New Testament in *2 Corinthians 3:18, But we all, with unveiled face, beholding as in a mirror the glory of the Lord, are being transformed into the same image from glory to glory.* Now I finally know what that means. I used to wonder about that verse. I get it, now. When you look in a mirror what do you see? You see your reflection, you see yourself. Now... by faith, looking in that reflection we see Jesus instead. Our identity is in Him. My righteousness will never be in myself; it is in Christ!"

She continued on her voice getting soft, "I kept wondering in my life, when am I going to be good enough? If I haven't read my Bible for a while or prayed....then I feel I can't come to God now and that I need to work harder at being a Christian. I just could never get close enough to God. I never felt good enough. I wanted to be that good Christian in my own mind, good enough to get my prayers answered. Well....," she sighed, her voice now gaining momentum, "It is not about me! It will never be about me! I will never be good enough. It's about Christ! My identity is in Christ! When I stand before God in prayer, I am standing in Him! I am standing in the righteousness of Jesus. I am clothed in Christ."

I was getting the sumo Jesus suit picture in my mind again. But I was starting to get really excited. What she was saying was really making sense to me. My life is like a three-ring circus that never stops, and I never have the time I want to spend to seek God, which makes me feel guilty when I come before Him. I was really tired of this and wondering when can I get closer to God? I wanted her to keep talking until I really grasped this concept, I needed this.

Carol went on, "When I come before the Father I come clothed in Jesus, I come in His righteousness to receive...... what the righteousness of Jesus has purchased for me, which is everything, from peace to healing to provision, everything! From head to toe I am provided for because from head to toe I am clothed in Christ!"

She stopped talking and there was silence on the telephone line. We were both overcome with emotion at the goodness of God. I couldn't wait to start praying in my own sumo Jesus suit. I felt my faith rising to new proportions. The focus was no longer on me and my poor performance but on Jesus and His perfect one, I am clothed in Christ.

Carol took a deep breath and began again. "Summer, there is more. There is this verse I have never understood; in fact, I didn't like it. It was after Jesus had fed the five thousand and the people were following Him because they wanted Him to feed them again.

Here I will read it to you, it is in *John 6:53-58 Then Jesus said to them, 'Most assuredly, I say to you, unless you eat the flesh of the Son of man and drink his blood you have no life within you. Whoever eats My flesh and drinks My blood has eternal life, and I will raise him up at the last day. For My flesh is food indeed and my blood is drink indeed. He who eats My flesh and drinks my blood abides in Me and I in him. As the living Father sent me, and I live because of the Father, so he who feeds on Me will live because of Me. This is the bread which came down from heaven—not as your fathers ate the manna and are dead. He who eats this bread will live forever."*

"After Jesus said that, a lot of His disciples turned back from following Him," Carol said then added, "these verses always troubled me."

"Me too" I told her, "It almost sounds like cannibalism and the people didn't understand. I wonder why Jesus worded it like that," I added hoping she had the answer.

"Yes" she said, "But if they would have only understood what He was saying. The passion behind it is incredible! If we eat His body and drink His blood, we will abide with Him. This isn't talking about communion; it is talking about a constant faith in what Jesus did at the cross. This is our food this is our drink. Our identity is in Christ. This is abiding in Him. This is our work, to believe in Jesus."

Carol continued explaining, "Earlier in this same chapter, when the crowd wanted Jesus to feed them again and He tells them in verse 27, not to work for the food that perishes but to work for the food that endures to everlasting life. Then the people ask Him, 'What shall we do that we may work the works of God?' I will quote His answer in verse 29 *Jesus answered and said to them, 'This is the work of God, that you believe in Him whom He sent.'* Do you see Summer? Our work is to believe. Our constant faith is to be in Jesus death and resurrection, and it is our food that endures unto eternal life. I used to think as believers we start at the cross and we move on from there."

Carol's voice was getting excited again, she was actually getting giddy and then she boldly proclaimed. "I will never get past the cross! I am talking about His death and His resurrection! I will live there! This is my food and drink! This is abiding in Him! It is a constant faith in what He has done for me."

Carol was starting to sound like an old-time gospel preacher, she was more shouting than talking as she finished. "The Bible says if we abide in Christ, we can ask what we will, and it will be done for us. Abiding in Christ is by faith! It is a constant feeding on Him and what He has done! When I lay hands on someone to pray for them, it is Jesus praying, because, by faith in His blood and His body, I am in Him! I stand as Christ! It is all Jesus. It is not my righteousness, not my own works!"

"But, Carol," I interrupted, "We can't be free to sin. I realize it is not our own righteousness, but we can't run around and sin there has to be balance here. After all, the Bible says, 'faith without works is dead.'"

"It is faith that takes us out of the law and crosses

us over to grace." Carol responded and added, "It is faith that sets us free from sin; it takes our focus off ourselves and onto Jesus. We can be free because of what Jesus has done. When we focus on ourselves and trying not to sin, it only causes us to sin. Focusing on Jesus and what He has done frees us."

My head was spinning; I was trying to digest all the wonderful things we discussed. Faith was now even more important because faith is the work of God in our lives, it is our job. Believing on Jesus blood and on His body is the food that endures to eternal life. We feed on Him by faith, this is abiding in Christ. We are clothed in Christ. We stand as Christ. We come before the throne of God in Jesus righteousness, to receive by faith, what His righteousness has purchased for us. I could hear kids in the background trying to get Carol's attention.

"I have to go now, bye."

"Bye" I said, and I was glad she called.

Chapter Seven

Abraham the Father of Faith

And if you are Christ's then you are Abraham's seed, and heirs according to the promise. Galatians 3:29

Ring, ring, my telephone rang.

"Hello" I answered, wondering who would be calling so early in the morning. I get up around six to get ready for work.

"Summer!" My sister Carol cried, there was so much emotion in her voice I couldn't tell if she was laughing or crying.

"Are you okay?" I asked concerned.

"Yes, I just can't believe the things God is showing me. It is so awesome!"

"Well tell me." I couldn't wait to hear.

"Well," she began, "I was lying in bed thinking about the things God showed me a few months ago and I asked Him for more. I said 'God, please give me more revelation, show me more.' And this is what He said, it just blew me away.

He said, 'Most people think Satan is the rival and equal opposite of Jesus, but he's not. Satan's opposite is Abraham!"

"Abraham!" I was shocked. "Tell me more."

"Yes Abraham," Carol was so excited she was almost breathless. "Think of its Summer, Satan is just an angel he is not Jesus' opposite, Jesus is God."

But how does Abraham fit in?" I asked her. I knew the story of Abraham well, it is found in Genesis, chapters 12-25. Genesis is my favorite book in the Bible, I have read it more than any other book. I knew the story of Abraham well, but I had no idea what she was talking about.

Well, to begin with," Carol said, "Satan came from a place of total light and living in God's glory, he was the highest angel in heaven, from there he went to a place of total disobedience. Satan became the tempter which caused the human race to fall into sin and a place of hopelessness. On the other hand, Abraham came from a place of total darkness but moved into a place of total obedience to God, and God told him through his obedience all the nations of the world would be blessed."

I thought of the story of Abraham. God called Abraham from the land of Ur. That truly was a place of total darkness, a godless land of idolatry. God called Abraham away from his own people to a land God promised to give to Abraham's ancestors. The land was Israel and Abraham's ancestors were the Jewish people.

One of the most amazing parts of Abraham's story

was that he was childless, and God promised him a son, In fact, God promised Abraham as many descendants as the stars in the sky and the sand by the seashore. The only problem was Abraham was ninety-nine and his wife was ninety, they had gotten too old to have any children. Even though it looked impossible the Bible tells us that Abraham believed God and it was credited to him as righteousness. This is why Abraham is called the father of faith.

Although Abraham moved to the promised land he never settled down. He lived in a tent and traveled as a nomad. But the most amazing thing about Abraham's story was Abraham's complete obedience and love for God. When Abraham finally received his son that God had promised him, a boy he named Isaac, God asked Abraham to sacrifice his son to Him. Isaac was thirteen at the time. Abraham brought him to a mountain that God had showed him, and he bound Isaac, his dear, beloved son, and laid him on the altar and lifted his hand with a knife to sacrifice him. But God called from heaven and stopped him. God was so pleased with Abraham's willingness to sacrifice his son that He makes Abraham a promise.

It is in *Genesis 22:16-18* *"By Myself I have sworn, says the Lord, because you have done this thing and not withheld your son, your only son, in blessing I will bless you and in multiplying I will multiply your descendants as the stars of the heaven and as the sand which is on the seashore; and your descendants shall possess the gates of their enemies. In your seed all the nations of the earth shall be blessed, because you have obeyed My voice."*

Back to Carol and our phone call.

"Tell me more," I prompted Carol again.

"Remember we heard once, the teaching that God had to have someone's faith for Him to legally move on earth? Well, Abraham's faith is what brought Jesus to earth."

My mind was searching for everything I knew about Abraham. I could see that the fact that Abraham was willing to sacrifice his only son for God was amazingly similar to God sacrificing His only son for us. I had a suspicion this strange request from God had something to do with Jesus.

Carol continued, "Think of Abraham's life, Summer, what three things stand out that Abraham believed for?"

"The birth of his son," I answered stating the obvious one.

"Yes" Carol confirmed. "Abraham believed for a supernatural birth. He also believed for a resurrection from the dead."

"Do you mean when he was willing to sacrifice Isaac?" I was thinking of the verse in Hebrews that talked about Abraham and Isaac. *By faith Abraham when he was tested, offered up Isaac, and he who had received the promises offered up his only begotten son, of whom it was said, "in Isaac your seed shall be called.' Accounting that God was able to raise him up even from the dead from which He also had received him in a figurative sense. Hebrews 11:17-18*

"Well yes, there is that, but Abraham believed for Jesus resurrection!"

"What!" I couldn't remember that in the Bible.

"Bear with me," Carol said. "Remember in Hebrews the seventh chapter when it talks about Levi the priest paying tithes. And it is referring to Abraham who paid tithes and Levi was still in his loins, or otherwise wasn't born yet?"

I thumbed through my Bible to the chapter and found the verse and found it. "Here it is" I said and read it to her. *"Even Levi, who receives tithes, paid tithes through Abraham, so to speak, for he was still in the loins of his father when Melchizedek met him." {Hebrews 7:9-10}*

"So you see that even though Levi was not yet born, the Bible referred to him as in the loins of Abraham," Carol explained. Then she asked me, "If Levi was in the loins of Abraham where was the physical body of Jesus?"

"The same as Levi, not yet born in Abraham's seed," I answered.

"The Bible tells us Abraham's seed was dead. Abraham believed for his seed to be resurrected!" Carol was getting excited again. "Don't you see it Summer, Abraham by faith resurrected Jesus, through his seed, two thousand years ahead of time, he believed for Jesus resurrection!!!"

"That reminds me of *Hebrews 3:16*," I told Carol. *"Now to Abraham and his Seed were the promises made. He does not say, 'And to seeds' as of many, but as of one, 'And to your Seed,' who is Christ.* The Bible tells us Abraham's seed was Christ."

"So, Abraham believed for a supernatural birth and a resurrection from the dead. He also believed for something else, a city," Carol said. "Abraham never actually lived in Jerusalem he wandered around in a tent. He never received the city he was believing for while he was on earth."

"That's right" I said thumbing through my Bible. I knew this part was in the Bible too. "*Hebrews 11: 8-9*" I said and began to read, "*By faith Abraham obeyed when he was called to go out to the place he would receive as an inheritance. And he went out not knowing where he was going. By faith he sojourned in the land of promise as in a foreign country, dwelling in tents with Isaac and Jacob, the heirs with him of the same promise; for he waited for the city who has foundations, whose builder and maker is God.*"

"Abraham believed for heaven!" Carol cried. "Do you see it? Remember when Jesus was talking about heaven in Luke 16:22 in the story of the rich man and Lazarus? Jesus called paradise, Abraham's bosom. It was Abraham's place! Abraham also believed for heaven!"

"Wow!" I said. "Satan's nemesis is Abraham, Abraham believed for Jesus' birth and resurrection, and heaven! No wonder he is called the father of faith."

"Yes" Carol continued, "but not only are the Jews the children of Abraham, so are we, those who believe. We, like Abraham, are those who are saved through faith. When God showed Abraham the stars in the sky and told him that is how many descendants, he would have he was also referring to those who would believe, those who would have faith, like Abraham did. It is right here in *Galatians 3:19, And if you are Christ's then you are*

Abraham's seed and heirs according to the promise."

Carol said more, "Satan thought he had legally taken the earth from God but, through Abraham's faith, God was able to restore it, to those, who like Abraham, believe God." Then Carol added, "Who has Satan persecuted on the earth, but the Jews and the Christians."

"Abraham's seed," I said, realizing now, for the first time just why Satan hated these two groups of people so much, "It was by faith that Abraham was made righteous and now we are made righteous by faith in the body and blood of Christ."

"I have to go," Carol said.

"I do too," I said looking at the clock, it was time for me to go to work.

Volume Three

Secret of Faith

Chapter Eight
The Secret of Faith

Now behold one came and said to Him, "Good Teacher what good thing shall I do that I may have eternal life?" So, He said to him, "Why do you call Me good? No one is good but One, that is God." Matthew 19:16-17

For he who comes to God must believe that He is, and that He is a rewarder of those who diligently seek Him Hebrews 10:6

Are you ready for the secret to faith? Shhhhhhhh! Listen, here it is.........

This is the secret of faith, to know that God is good, and that He is a rewarder of those who diligently seek Him. That is it! That's the secret!

God is good! He is GOOD, GOOD, GOOD! Through faith, in Jesus we have right standing with God, Our Father. God is good, you can trust Him. He is not mad at you. He has good things planned for you. He loves you. You can trust Him. He has not forgotten you. He knows what you are going through. He hears you when you call. You can trust Him. He is able to take care of you. He is great. He is powerful. He is eternal, and you can trust Him.

In fact, there is no one else you can trust completely. There is only One who is good and that is God. If you are trusting your parents, they may let you down. If you are trusting your mate, they may let you down. If you are trusting your money or friends or your children or God forbid the government, they may fail you. Even if you are trusting yourself, you are not on solid ground. Only God is good. Only God is able. Only God is completely trustworthy, and He will never let you down.

The secret of faith is to have it in God! He is the only one anywhere that you can completely trust. He is able to help you; He is willing to help you. Trust Him! Trust Him! Trust Him!

Does this sound too simple? Just to believe God is good. Satan works overtime to get people to believe the opposite. He is good at it. People blame God for everything, loved one's premature deaths, sickness, accidents, tornadoes, hurricanes, unanswered prayers, etc. etc. etc... Why do to think Satan works so hard to get you to blame God? He doesn't want you to have faith!!!!

Even those of us who know the Lord, have areas in our lives we feel that God has let us down. This is not true. There are things we just don't understand yet, but we are given a clue in the Lord's Prayer. The part where it says, "Your kingdom come, Your will be done on earth as it is in heaven."

God's kingdom hasn't come to earth at this time. Satan has a kingdom set up here. Satan and his fallen angels and also fallen mankind, bring chaos to the earth. But God's will is being done in heaven. They don't have accidents there and no one is sick, no one suffers any kind of pain, and every need is met. It is a wonderful place of unbelievable delights, because our good God's will is done there.

Summer's Tips on Faith

I want to give you a little tip from Summer on faith. Focus on what God has done for you already. And refuse to stop believing that God is good and that He will come through for you. Diligently seek Him. Do not believe anything else. Don't even believe circumstances. Sometimes it seems God isn't coming through. I have been through those times. Sometimes it seems like He's forgotten me. I have thought that before. I am older now, I know better. Trust Him. He is still there, and He knows what He is doing.

Summer's Foundation Shaken

There were so many times I went through a hard time and wondered where God was, not knowing He knew what was best for me. He hadn't deserted me, and I was still in His loving care. There was no way I could see it at the time. I will tell you of one such time, but there are many.

When I was seventeen, I went through an especially hard time at the end of my second year of High School. I went through a time I felt betrayed by my friends. It was a time of misunderstandings.

I remember thinking to myself, "Who needs friends anyway, I have my parents."   Only to have my parents disappoint me too. It was nothing earth shattering but for my delicate emotional balance of my teen years it was devastating. It caused me to go through a mild rebellion. It upended me and shook me up. What I didn't know was, that God was doing what was best for me and He was right there with me all the time.

I remember that day, my girlfriend Laurie was moving away. I felt she was my last friend on earth. Especially since my parents had joined the ranks of those, I felt betrayed me.

Laurie was from another town. She had been extremely wild and rebellious, which had contributed to a nervous breakdown for her mother. Laurie's father had no alternative but to put her in foster care while her mother recuperated. Her foster home was in my town, and she went to my high school; we became friends. Foster care had been good for Laurie; she had been placed in a preacher's home and had become a Christian, although she was still on the wild side. We had been friends and now she was leaving.

My other friends and my own parents had failed me, and my last friend was leaving. My fragile emotional state was shattered, and I was devastated.

Where was God? Didn't He care? Why was this happening to me?

I was sobbing away, and Laurie was puffing on a cigarette, listening to my misery.

"Ya wanna smoke?" she asked.

"Yah," I answered, and took a puff, thinking how mad I was at my parents. Smoking was something I had given to the Lord when I got saved. It was my first little backslide. It started a period of upheaval in me, and it took several years to quit smoking again. I wondered why God let it happen because I wanted to serve Him, but I felt I got slammed. Things that were important to me, {a very immature seventeen-year-old} stacked up against me to the point I broke down.

Years later I asked the Lord about it. I knew I had been immature, but it seemed that He had let my life fall apart and I had been so hurt and that it shouldn't have happened that way. "Lord, why did I go through all of that?" I asked thinking back to that time in my life, "Where were you?"

The Lord answered me, and His answer surprised me. "I saw what was coming in your life, Summer. I was preparing you."

Suddenly I knew what He was talking about. Two years later, when I was nineteen, my parents divorced. It was the hardest and most painful thing I had ever been through. I cried myself to sleep every night afterward for at least a year. It was like having the ground pulled out from under my feet.

"I had to prepare you for what was coming, or I would have lost you then," the Lord continued to explain. "Your security wasn't in Me; it was in your parent's marriage."

What the Lord was saying was true. My early childhood had been devastating. I had a single mother who was always at work. My twin sister and I never felt safe. We had been hurt many times, abused by those who watched us, and we had given up inside. We were like two leaves tossed in the wind emotionally.

Then my mother began dating someone wonderful. My sister and I fell in love with him too. When my mom married my dad, my life changed. You cannot imagine the relief I felt the day they got married.

I remember saying to myself, "It's over." Now I had a dad and a stay-at-home mom. It was a relief. Like the feeling when a war was over. My security, in my life, was placed in their marriage. It became my foundation.

"I had you go through similar emotions two years ahead of time, so you would transfer your trust to Me. Also, you were so compliant, if you hadn't been slightly rebellious; you would have never married Jim, my choice for you."

I was amazed. Tears filled my eyes and my heart burned. I couldn't believe it! I couldn't have been more wrong. I had thought the Lord had deserted me, but I was mistaken.

I couldn't believe the loving care and the planning the Lord had done in my life! He was preparing me for what was ahead. He had looked ahead and thought it all through and chose the way that He thought was best for me. Even though the divorce was very difficult for me, I had been prepared. He didn't lose me because He had prepared me ahead of time.

His love for me overwhelmed me. The time I had thought He wasn't there for me had been just the opposite! He gently and carefully has handled me through the years as though I was the most precious commodity in the world.

Sometimes it takes years to see.

I was realizing something. I can trust Him! His love is so great I can trust Him! There are some things I can't understand at the time, I just leave them on the shelf for now, someday, I will understand, but I know I can trust Him.

He is my foundation now. I am stronger now because I am on the firm foundation that can't be moved. It took some pain to move me, but He did what was best for me!

He is bigger than me, He is more powerful than me and He is definitely smarter than I am. He can see my future; He knows what is coming and He is preparing the way. I CAN trust Him!

I want you to learn something from my thirty-eight years of serving the Lord. God is good. He loves you. He is carefully, lovingly preparing you for what is ahead. You will not understand everything, but you need to hold onto this. GOD IS GOOD! HE LOVES YOU! YOU CAN TRUST HIM! Diligently seek Him, He will reward you. This is the basis for my faith.

Now, when you just read that, did you have a problem with it?

Did a little voice say to you, God loves her, but He doesn't love me?

Or did you think, God had never come through for me?

If He loved me, I wouldn't be in this mess I am in. My life is miserable and it will always be miserable, God never helps me. She is just special.

No, no, no, no!

I am talking to you.

We have to have our faith in God. We can't trust in our parents, or our mates, or our money or God forbid the government. Your trust, your faith, your security needs to be in GOD! He is your foundation. Remember, He is, and He is a rewarder of those who diligently seek Him. {me and you}

Chapter Nine

Satan the Enemy of Faith

"The thief does not come except to steal, and to kill, and to destroy."   John 10:10

Satan is God's enemy. The reason I am talking about the devil in a book about faith is because he doesn't want you to have faith. He is constantly working to destroy your trust in God. And, if you are holding onto faith, he will oppose you and try to get you out of faith. I want to get to the bottom of some of the reasons people lose faith in God.

Although Satan was once a servant of God, he has fallen from heaven. He knows his doom is coming and he wants to do as much harm as he can to God before his eternal doom. Satan cannot possibly hurt God, so he unleashes his fury on humans knowing God's great love for them and he especially despises those who serve God and bring Him joy. Because we serve God, God's enemy is our enemy. We are Satan's target, and he wants to destroy us.

Satan comes to steal, kill and destroy us. If you live on earth, you will encounter the devil and he will try to steal you from God.

Satan will try to get you to believe a lie. Many, many people fall for Satan's lies about God. Satan will bring tragedy into people's life just to get you to lose faith in God. Then he whispers in their ear, "Why would you serve a God who let your mother die?" Or "Where was God when your father abused you?"

Or if he can't get you to believe God is not good, he will tell you that you are no good. He will convince you that you are worthless, and God does not want you. Which is completely opposite from the truth. He would not work so hard to keep you from God if this was true. Satan knows your tremendous value to God and that is why he has convinced you that you are worthless. {If you think you are worthless because of the sin in your life, remember, God has already taken care of that problem}

Satan convinces people God is not good and

that God does not care. He gets masses of people to turn their backs on God in ignorance. When Satan successfully feeds people a lie, he robs them of their faith and a close walk with God. It is his purpose to even rob them of their souls.

Who is really behind all these evil things? It is Satan himself and he gets his help from us. Let us talk about some of the reasons bad things happen.

Sin

Sin will give Satan legal rights into people's lives, not just individuals but whole families. The unseen world operates by certain laws and Satan knows them well. If Satan is successful and he can get you to sin, he will accuse you before God and demand certain rights. When those in authority, like fathers and mothers give in to sin, Satan will attack their children. This is called generational curses. The evil that comes on those who take Satan's bait does not come from God. The good news is Jesus has paid the price for our sin and we may repent and be set free.

Generational Curses

Generational curses can ruin people's lives. Some people are born into trouble. They are born into abusive homes, alcoholic homes, sexually abusive homes, poverty-stricken homes and more. It seems they start off in this world with hardly a chance. A generational curse can be anything you can think of from infertility to cancer to promiscuity. Anywhere that Satan has gotten a foothold in a family line. And it seems that some inherit unbelievable problems. The answer of course is to fight it, through your walk with the Lord. Any generational curse can end with you! But this is one of the ways Satan promotes evil on the earth. Through sins which cause him to get a foothold in families, called generational curses.

False Religions

False religions can give Satan a stronghold over whole countries. Poverty sickness and diseases not to mention child trafficking and many other horrors, are predominant in countries Satan rules through false religions. Choosing to follow false gods, which is really to follow Satan, shuts God out. Which shuts out everything good. It actually gives Satan legal rights. That is why we see nations with false gods in such bad shape. We can't look at the world and blame God for this mess. Through false religions Satan can come against whole countries and people groups and bring wars to the earth.

Faith, in a Dark World

I choose to follow Christ.

I choose to come out from under the authority of Satan and his evil kingdom and his curses. I choose this by choosing to follow Jesus and come under His authority.

I choose to obey God. I choose to believe God.

When something happens, I don't understand, when it may seem God has failed me, I know that God is good and whatever I am going through I can trust Him.

I refuse to fall for Satan's lies. <u>God is good</u> and He will reward me because I diligently seek Him! This is the truth.

When we begin to move in faith, we can expect the devil to oppose us. In fact, when you begin to grow as a Christian you can expect the devil to oppose you. This shows you that faith is worth fighting for! Faith is a big deal. When you begin walking in faith in an area in your life, it will not just affect you, it will affect others.

Think of it like this, that we on this earth are surrounded by invisible walls of darkness that hold us back. These are Satan's strongholds. When you begin to walk in faith in an area of your life, such as healing, deliverance, divine protection, provision, leading others to Jesus, etc. etc., you are punching a hole in this wall which makes a way for others to follow. You are doing damage to Satan's kingdom and someone behind you will benefit. They will follow you to freedom, through the opening, you have created.

I remember when my sister and I were fifteen years old. We had heard about the baptism of the Holy Spirit and speaking in tongues. We wanted this! For months we wanted this more than anything, but our church did not believe in such things. In fact, they would show you the door if you mentioned them. When we moved to a new town that year, my sister and I finally got our parents to visit a church that believed in such things. It was our secret hope that somehow, we could get what these people had. This was our chance. I kept praying all through the service, "Lord please have them pray for people who want the baptism in the Holy Spirit, after the service."

It was a lively service, not what we were used to, the atmosphere was charged with the power of God. Then the Pastor dismissed the service. I was so disappointed. I was just too shy to go forward and ask for prayer in a strange church, in a strange town, unless he particularly called for that thing.

The Pastor dismissed the service and started to walk away from the microphone. My heart sank.

Then he stopped, he stood there for a

second and then he turned and went back and announced, "If anyone here would like to receive the Baptism in the Holy Spirit you can come forward for prayer."

That was all we needed. My sister and I went forward and asked for prayer. Several altar workers took us in the back and prayed for us. We joined hands and stood in a circle to pray. They led us in a prayer. As we were praying my sister, Carol, actually heard an audible voice say, "Nothing happened."

She opened her eyes to look and see who said it. Everyone in the circle had their eyes closed in prayer. She realized the voice was from the devil. After the prayer we were instructed to expect, in faith, our new prayer language to come.

The devil was not happy about this at all. First the voice Carol heard and next, we had another surprise. Our parents were angry. They were so angry at us when we came out of the prayer room, we couldn't find them anywhere. They had left us and went home! Here we were in a strange town we had just moved to and we didn't even know how to get home. We had to ask a complete stranger for a ride home. At least we could give them our address. Once we got home our parents were still angry. I had never seen them act like this. The devil really didn't want this to happen.

A week or two later I was lying in bed at night, wondering when I would speak in tongues, when some words came to my mind. "Abba kee alla weya." I tried saying them out loud, but they were hard to pronounce. My hands seemed to float up in the air as I said them, and I felt a strangely wonderful, peaceful feeling. I was lying on my back in bed with my hands in the air, trying to pronounce this sentence that came to my head, when a strong thought hit me. "You are just making that up," it said. I didn't realize then it was the devil.

"Oh," I said to myself. "I must have made that up." I stopped. Then I answered myself, "I don't care if I did make that up or not, it felt wonderful!" I started to say the phrase again when a stream of words came flooding from my mouth and this time the words were not hard to pronounce. I was speaking in tongues! I ran to my sister Carol's room; it took all my effort to speak in English, my mouth just wanted to flow in another language.

"I want it too!" my sister cried. And that was her last English word. A marvelous flood of tongues came from her too. My breakthrough had caused her breakthrough.

For months we would rush home after school, run up to our rooms and pray for hours. It was wonderful. Our parents came around too. In fact, my dad became a part of a full gospel men's group that brought full gospel speakers to our area.

Satan is the enemy of our faith. He does not want us to receive from God. He will oppose you as he did my sister, Carol and me. Don't let him stop you from receiving in faith. And my breakthrough caused Carol also to receive from God, and later our parents.

Remember, Satan is God's enemy. He keeps people deceived about God. He is behind the evil and injustice on the earth and he successfully gets people to blame God, the answer to their problems. In this way he even steals people's souls. We need to look past his lies and not allow him to mar our view of God. We need to move out in faith and not allow him to deceive us out of receiving from God.

 If you have felt God was unjust in some way, maybe you have swallowed one of Satan's cleverly crafted lies to keep you from God.

It is time to let that go. The truth will set you free.

The truth is **God is good!**

Chapter Ten

Our Responsibility

Every good gift and every perfect gift is from above, and comes down from the Father of lights, with whom there is no variation or shadow of turning. James1:17

I want to talk about our responsibilities of faith. Many people have the mistaken idea that God can do anything, therefore everything that happens is His will and also His fault. This is not true. God does not just do whatever He feels like doing, whenever He feels like doing it, just because He is God. There are some things that God cannot do. He cannot go against His own word. He obeys His own laws, and He only does things that are legal. He cannot help you in an illegal way. God is righteous, God is just, God is completely legal, and He deals with everyone in a legal way, even Satan.

God had given the responsibility, to rule on earth,

to Adam. This means it was no longer legally God's. Satan by deception stole Adam's authority and became ruler of this world. Satan now had a legal right to operate on earth. But God did not throw in the towel and desert us. He sent Jesus on earth to redeem us. Jesus had to come in human form. Jesus overcame Satan through death and resurrection and now through faith in Jesus we have been purchased back in a legal way. Faith is the key word. Everything we do as Christians is through faith. The Bible says we are saved through faith.

Faith in what? Faith in Jesus, through His death and resurrection. We come out of Satan's authority by coming under Jesus' authority through faith.

Does Satan have some legal rights? Yes, he seems to. We see this in scripture. There seems to be some sort of courtroom in heaven where Satan presents himself and demands from God what he feels is his, and he also accuses us and demands rights over us when we sin. And then sometimes for no reason at all except we please God he petitions God to test us. We see this in the first chapter of Job. Satan comes before God and petitions God that he may severely test Job. Even though God and Satan are enemies, Satan seems to legally have some standing where he is able to present himself before God, against mankind.

We are also given hints of this elsewhere. Remember in Luke 22:31, Jesus tells Peter that Satan had asked to have him to sift him as wheat. Satan had presented his case against Peter; Jesus had also been there and interceded for Peter.

This was some sort of legal debate that was had over Peter. Obviously, Satan was able to legally demand something because Peter went through a trial, and he denied the Lord three times.

We see the end of Satan's legal seat in heaven is coming soon. The Bible tells us in, *Revelation12:7-10 And war broke out in heaven: Michael and his angels fought against the dragon; and the dragon and his angels fought, but they did not prevail, nor was a place found for them in heaven any longer. So, the great dragon was cast out, that serpent of old, called the devil and Satan, who deceives the whole world; he was cast to the earth, and his angels were cast out with him. Then I heard a loud voice saying in heaven, "Now salvation and strength, and the kingdom of our God, and the power of His Christ have come, for the accuser of our brethren, who accused them day and night, has been cast down.*

So, we see Satan has some judicial place in heaven at this time and he uses it to continually accuse us before God. I also believe there have been some serious arguments over souls as they die. Satan tries to claim souls he has gotten to sin. {We need to know that Satan no longer has a legal right to us the believer, we are translated out of his kingdom. But he does still have a kingdom of darkness on the earth, the unredeemed mankind, are still under his authority, and he still has some judicial rights before God.}

God does things legally and in order and He has delegated to us some legal responsibilities that He will not do for us. We have to do them. This is where a lot of people lose faith. They want God to do everything, and they do not take responsibility for their part.

Before Jesus left earth, He imparted the church, or the believers on earth, His authority here. He told us in *Matthew 28:18 "All authority has been given to Me in heaven and earth."* Then Jesus begins to delegate that authority to the church. We are mandated to preach the Gospel to the ends of the earth, and we are given authority in Mark 16:16 -18 to cast out demons, to heal the sick, to speak with new tongues and power over poisonous things. Jesus is delegating legal authority here. Through Jesus we have been given some legal rights! There is much more. The Bible tells us in Ephesians 3:12 we have access before God with boldness and confidence! In fact, anywhere in the New Testament where you read the words, 'in Him 'these are our legal rights! They belong to us through faith in Him! But we also have the responsibility to use them; we can't sit around and expect God to do our job for us.

I find a passage in Kenneth Hagin's book, *I Believe In Visions,* very fascinating. I consider Kenneth Hagin the most outstanding teacher on faith in our time. This portion of this passage helps us to see the point of our authority and responsibilities on earth. In this passage, Kenneth is in a vision and conversing with Jesus. Jesus is teaching Kenneth about dealing with demons, I will quote to you what happens next.

While Jesus was talking to me, an evil spirit ran up between me and Jesus and spread out something that looked like a cloud or a smoke screen. I couldn't

see Jesus anymore. Then the demon began to jump up and down, waving his arms and legs and yelling in a shrill voice, "Yackety, yack, yack, yack." I paused for a moment. I could hear the voice of Jesus as He continued to talk to me, but I could not understand what He was saying. I could hear His voice but could not distinguish the words.

I thought to myself, "Doesn't the Lord know that I am missing what He is saying? I need to get that it is important, but I am missing out on it." I wondered why Jesus didn't command the evil spirit to stop. I waited for a few more minutes. Jesus continued talking as if He didn't even know that the evil spirit was present. I wondered why the Lord didn't cast him out, but He didn't.

Finally, I grew tired of it. I pointed my finger at the evil spirit and said, "I command you in the name of Jesus Christ to be quiet!" He stopped immediately and fell to the floor. The black smoke screen disappeared, and I could see Jesus once again. The evil spirit lay on the floor whimpering and whining like a whipped pup. I said, "Not only must you be quiet but get up and get out of here." He got up and ran away.

I was still wondering why Jesus did not stop this evil spirit from interfering as he did, and of course Jesus knew what I was thinking. He said, "If you hadn't done something about that I couldn't have."

"Lord, I know I misunderstood you. You said You couldn't do anything about it, but You really meant that You wouldn't."

"No," He said, "If you hadn't done something

about that spirit, I couldn't."

"But Lord, You can do anything. To say that you couldn't is different than anything that I have ever heard preached or that I ever preached myself. That really upends my theology."

I am going to stop there I wanted you to see that Jesus told Kenneth that He couldn't have done anything. In the dialogue, Jesus goes onto explain that He has delegated that authority to the church and gives several scriptures. Jesus also tells Kenneth nowhere does it tell us to pray against the devil. It usually says to "rebuke" or "resist" or "give no place to" the devil, which is because as believers in Jesus, through Jesus we have been delegated this authority on earth. We have to know God's legal system. We have to know what our responsibilities are, and we can't, out of lack of knowledge, blame God for not doing His part. GOD ALWAYS DOES HIS PART. If there is a failure on someone's part, it is on the human side or a lack of understanding.

I learned a lesson from God when I was a young wife and mother, during one of the hardest periods of my life. My husband couldn't get steady work and we were broke. He had also got into trouble with the law and was facing a lengthy prison sentence. We were at the bottom and needed everything. I had a long prayer list. During this period, I had an experience with God. A veil pulled back, and I was standing before Him. I was never so presently surprised. He was my Father and I had never felt more accepted or at home anywhere or at any time in my life. Suddenly I remembered my life and what a mess I was in.

Here I was standing before God, and I had great favor. I started to ask for all the things I needed. He stopped me immediately. He would not even discuss it. He explained to me that every need I had; He had already met. In fact, every need that anyone has He has already made arrangements for each need. Everything I needed, He explained to me, was already available. It was up to me to receive it by faith. The responsibility was on me.

Faith is like a giant arm that reaches up to heaven and pulls down our answer. It releases angels. It brings healing. It brings provision. It brings us the answers we need. Yes, if we step out in faith, we will have a struggle with the enemy. The devil will try to block your answer, steal your provision or at least slow it down. But as for God's part, it is done. Any need you have He has made provision for it.

I want to boost your faith with a testimony from a young man who toured heaven and saw first-hand that God has storehouses in heaven with provisions for those on earth. This young man was only eight years old when Jesus showed him a tour of heaven. His name is Roberts Liardon. He records his vision in a little book called *I Saw Heaven.* I will quote you a passage.

We walked a little farther- and this is the most important part of my story. I saw three storage houses 500 to 600 yards from the Throne Room of God. They're very long and very wide. There may be more, but I only saw three. We walked into the first. As Jesus shut the front door behind us, I looked around the interior in shock!

On one side of the building were arms, fingers and other exterior parts of the body. Legs hung from the wall, but the scene looked natural, not weird. On the other side of the building were shelves filled with neat little packages of eyes: green ones, brown ones, blue ones etc.

This building contained all the parts of the human body that people on earth need, but they haven't realized these blessings are waiting for them in heaven. There is no place else in the universe for these parts to go except right here on earth; no one else needs them. And they are for saints and sinners alike.

Jesus said to me, "These are the unclaimed blessings. This building should not be full. It should be emptied every single day. You should come in here with faith and get the needed parts for you and the people you'll come in contact with that day."

Those unclaimed blessings are there in those storehouses—all the parts of the body people might need: hundreds of new eyes and legs, skin, hair ear drums--- they're all there. All you have to do is go in and get what you need by the arm of faith, because it's there, it's there, it's there.

God has made a legal way for us to receive from Him; it is through faith, faith in Jesus. The sacrifice of Jesus made the door to heaven open to us. We need to receive from God in this way, His way, faith. Whining and complaining and crying and trying to make God feel sorry for you does not work. You don't even have to try that stuff, I already have, it doesn't work. Receiving by faith in what? In Jesus, His sacrifice, a legal purchase, this is the legal way to receive our legal rights in Him.

We have a responsibility to do our part, through faith, to change things. God has already made the provision we need. Don't sit around and wait for God to move when He has already equipped you for the job. Think of our story, about Kenneth Hagin, how he was waiting for Jesus to do something about the evil spirit who was interfering with their conversation. Kenneth waited for Jesus to do something, and when He didn't, Kenneth very simply rebuked the demon and it left. Kenneth could do it because Jesus had delegated that authority to the believers.

People blame God for the condition of the earth. "It must be God's will." They will say about everything. They misunderstand their own responsibility. It is up to us to appropriate God's will for our lives and our homes and then in our world. We do this by faith.

I also want to make one last point at the end of this chapter. I have been wondering where to put this point so I will put it here. If you haven't made the commitment to God, that your life is in His hands, then to some extent, in your life, God's hands are tied. You can't expect everything that happens to you to be in His plan. We need to surrender ourselves to God. To the extent we are surrendered to Him, that is the extent He can work in our lives.

Also, if you are disobedient to God and refuse to follow His direction for you, you are bound to get into trouble. People do this and then when tragedy happens, they blame God, misunderstanding that they are the ones at fault. It is like running out in the middle of traffic and wondering why you got hit by a car.

You will be as close to God as you choose to be. The way is open. The level of commitment He has to you is decided by the level of commitment you have to Him. If you want to be in the place, in your life, that God has complete control, then you need to put yourself in that place. How do we put ourselves in that place? We need a complete commitment to God. That way you can know, God has your situation. At any point in our life, we can make this commitment. If you have gotten yourself into trouble, it is the perfect time! Remember the verse about faith, that God is a rewarder of those who diligently seek Him. We can't expect our lives to be in God's hands if we are not diligently seeking Him! We have some responsibilities to follow.

The level of our commitment to God is the level of God's ability to move in your life.

Things happen in our lives that we sometimes don't understand. This is no reason to lose faith or turn back. We have to press on into God and know that He is still good and some things we won't understand. That does not change God's character. God sees a bigger picture than we will ever see, we can trust Him. We need to do our part. God has delegated some authority and responsibilities to us that means if we don't do them, they won't get done.

Chapter Eleven
We Don't Understand Everything

"For My thoughts are not your thoughts, Nor are your ways My ways," says the Lord. "For as the heavens are higher than the earth, So are my ways higher than your ways, And my thoughts than your thoughts." Isaiah 55:8-9

There are times when things may happen that we don't understand. It is important during those times that we do not allow our faith in God to fail. If I do not understand something I like to, "put it on the shelf." That means I leave it alone until I can understand it. It may take a long time. What we don't want to do is decide that God failed us because things did not go the way we thought they should have. We have to remember that we do not understand everything! God does. I have had things on the shelf for many years before I understood them, and some things are still on the shelf. I will leave them there until I can understand them, but I will not lose my faith in God.

I say this now, but my faith in God has been tested through the years. I had nothing in my life but my faith, the faith that I was where God wanted me to be in life. It was an invisible cord that I was holding onto, that no one else could see or understand but me and that only faintly. I tell about my life in my book *The Impossible Marriage.*

I married my husband Jim believing with all my heart that He was God's choice for me. I was such a dysfunctional person that any choice for my life would probably been difficult, but marrying my husband was just plain impossible. I met my husband shortly after he had gotten paroled for the second time. His entire life was filled with abuse, violence and he had spent most of his life institutionalized in one form or another, juvenile homes, detention centers, county jails, rehab centers and ultimately prison. He was aptly described by one prison psychiatrist as "trouble waiting for a place to happen."

Although Jim was caught in the revolving doors in the prison system, he was a Christian and loved the Lord but seemed to be unable to carry out a Christian lifestyle. I have never seen another person on earth who has captured the Lord's heart like my husband has. To pray for my husband was like touching God's heart. He would answer many times audibly. My sister told me she asked the Lord about it one time because she would pray for Jim also. She asked the Lord why He spoke so clearly when she would pray for Jim. God told her, "Jim is on my priority list.

He is like the one sheep I have left the ninety-nine others to find."

When I married Jim, I literally stepped out of my boat of safety and began walking on a raging sea. My marriage was a walk of faith. I had trouble on every side. God immediately promised me a couple of things, while I was reading scripture early on in my marriage. One was that Jim would no longer go to prison. This was severely tested, we had many times he was standing before a judge facing felony charges through the years. God kept His promise, Jim was never sent back to prison. The other promise was for Jim's recovery emotionally and his ability to live without alcohol and drugs. I based my life on these two promises, and that God was in control of my life. I lived everyday walking on the water through the storm of living in a spiritual battle.

There were several times when I felt that God no longer had control of my life. That somehow things had gotten out of His control. I, like Peter, when he was walking on the water got my eyes on the size of the waves and immediately sunk. Two times when this happened, I literally went into shock and lost consciousness. The devastation I felt was so great. Had I deceived myself; was my whole life one big mistake?

The first time was when my husband had been arrested and was in the county jail. I didn't even know what he did or what he was being charged with. I tried to see him and couldn't. I tried to get him out on bond and the police told me that more charges were pending. I got my eyes off God's promises to me and thought things were too bad even for God to fix. I immediately felt myself sinking. My whole life was a mistake. I had deceived myself and God really wasn't in charge. I staggered to the bed, I felt myself going into shock. I went right through the bed and sunk into a deep black hole. I could feel myself falling. The pain and the shock that God really wasn't behind my life after all, was just too great, I believe I was dying.

At this point, Jesus audibly spoke to me, He said, "I am here." I returned to consciousness once He spoke. He was still in charge; He hadn't deserted me, and I hadn't deceived myself.

The second time was years later but similar. This time during a fight during my husband's drunkenness, the police were arresting me. I couldn't imagine what had happened to God and why He had left me, and this was happening to me. Again, I went into shock and lost consciousness. Again, I heard the audible voice of Jesus, and it brought me back to consciousness, this time He said, "You need to know how this feels."

Once He spoke, I knew He hadn't lost control. While I was going through this, it was His words and knowing there was a reason for what was happening, that got me through it. Even still, through the whole ordeal, I felt weak and shaken and barely conscious, like I would pass out at any minute. I still couldn't understand how when I was serving Him, that He could allow such a horrible thing to happen to me. Once I got home from jail, I didn't want to pray or even think about God for a few days. I just couldn't understand how He could do that to me. I was shaken up for months. I still don't quite understand the reason God wanted me to know how that felt. But I know He is good, and I trust Him. My life is His, to do with what He wants. We won't always understand everything. We can't let it turn us back or lose our faith. The day will come when we will understand that God's will was the best.

I read a wonderful book that illustrates this point. It is called *Appointments with Heaven* by Dr. Reggie Anderson. He tells in the book the story of his faith as a child. He had a close relationship with God as a small child. God was as real to him as anyone.

As he got older, Reggie's faith was severely shaken. In fact, he lost his faith. He had become very close to a wonderful Christian family. They were his distant cousins.

Beginning when he was ten years old Reggie began working with his uncle on a farm. Even at ten Reggie would stay alone at the farmers market, selling the watermelons his uncle grew. These were some of the happiest times of his life due to the Alday family, the family I mentioned that he had become close to. They sold watermelons in the next booth at the farmers market and kept an eye on young Reggie. The brothers were named Jimmy and Jerry and they sold the watermelons that their father Ned and other brother Chester would bring. Jimmy and Jerry were older than Reggie and they mentored him. And soon the oldest brother Jerry married a lovely girl named Mary. They taught him deep respect for God and how to treat women with respect. Reggie grew to love the Alday's as his own family and looked forward to his summers with them.

He worked in the farmers market with them from the time he was ten until he was sixteen. In his book he describes those summers with the Aldays at the market as, "Disneyland, the most happiest place on earth."

One day, in the spring while Reggie was in high school, his father showed up at the school, he had bad news for Reggie. The Alday family had been murdered. Jimmy and Jerry, Ned and Clark were found shot to death at Jerry's home. Jerry's wife Mary was found dead in the woods, she had seen her family murdered and then she had been raped and killed.

Reggie was more than devastated. He struggled back into class and waited for school to let out. After school that day Reggie ran deep into the woods and exploded; he screamed and kicked and beat at the trees and then he screamed at God, "Why did you let this happen? They loved you!!" Reggie's world was shattered he writes in his book.

I spent that summer at the market alone with my memories and frightened by my new ability to imagine evil. Sin had new depths, and depravity had new meaning. I had no protection from the darkness that lurked nearby.

My big brothers and earthly protectors were gone.

My heavenly Protector couldn't be trusted. God seemed useless to me now.

Reggie no longer had any use for God and no longer considered himself a believer, in fact, he no longer believed in God. Years went by and Reggie stayed away from God until he met a Christian girl in college, a girl who would have nothing to do with him because he was not a Christian. Reggie, still angry with God, went off on a trip into the wilderness. He took a copy of C.S. Lewis book, *Mere Christianity,* and a Bible. This trip would change his life. After Reggie read the book and The Gospel of John, Reggie fell asleep, and he woke up in heaven. I will quote some of the book.

Everything felt so real, more intense and tangible than my ordinary life. My senses seemed to awaken and open like a flower to the sun. I could see, hear, touch, smell and feel things like never before. I didn't feel like I was in a dream; I felt like this was the real life I'd always been searching for. This was more real than my life.

I spied a large rock nearby beyond the brook and perched on it to gaze on the magnificence displayed. Everything was so peaceful and serene, and I marveled at it all.

I didn't have time to think about how I'd gotten there because I heard an unmistakable voice calling me from the distance. It was the voice of someone I had once loved and who still loved me. It didn't make an audible sound; instead, it resonated inside me and echoed outside, as if I'd heard it with my heart, or maybe my soul. It was easily the most compelling yet comforting, voice I'd ever heard.

I spun to my right to glance at the person who had spoken to my heart, and I saw a great crowd of people moving toward me. As I scanned the crowd a cool breeze engulfed me. That's when I recognized them.

Jimmy, Jerry, Mary, Ned Chester and Aubrey!

I couldn't believe what I was seeing, but there was no mistaking them. They looked ecstatic. I'd never seen anyone as happy as they were. They didn't speak with words, but they seemed to know how much I had struggled with their deaths, and how that trauma had put up a barrier between God and me. In the most kind and loving way possible, they communicated that they weren't the obstacles to my faith. They were there to lift the burden I had been carrying around for so long.

I scanned their faces and could see only joy. Somehow, they made it clear that what had happened to them happened for a reason. They wanted me to know that I wouldn't fully understand until I joined them, but in the meantime, I shouldn't hold it against God. It took less than a millisecond for me to understand; this is where they belonged. They had no regrets about their departure from a fallen world. This wasn't their new spiritual home; this was their true corporeal home.

Reggie also sees Jesus.

"Reggie, why are you running from me?" Your friends are here with me in paradise; you can stop running. I am the one who came for you," He said.

Immediately I knew what He meant. For more than seven years I had been wandering aimlessly in a spiritual wilderness. He had come to rescue me from the hate and anger that had trapped me in that wasteland and to bring me back to the faith of my youth. He had come to restore me to Him.

Reggie lost faith in God because something

happened that he could not understand. He stopped believing God was good and that He cared. God became useless to Reggie because he saw the strong faith of his loved ones and yet they were murdered. Seeing them in heaven lifted his burden but still he was not told the reason why it happened. He was only told he wouldn't understand until he joined the Aldays in heaven.

It is important to remember that we will not understand many things about God and why things happen, in this lifetime. We have limited understanding here, and only see spiritual things dimly. The day will come when we understand but until then it is important to hang onto our faith in God and to never lose faith in Him, no matter how things look. Reggie's wonderful story continues, and he faces more hard things in his life, but he doesn't lose faith in God again. Reggie learned this most important thing, and so have I, and that is to trust God and that we won't understand everything that happens. That is okay. I will put what I don't understand on the shelf and leave it there until the day I will understand. But for now, I will not allow my faith in God to be shaken!

Volume Four

Principles of Faith

Chapter Twelve

Faith and Obedience

"And I will make your descendants multiply as the stars of the heavens; I will give to your descendants all these lands; and in your seed all the nations of the earth shall be blessed; Because Abraham obeyed my voice and kept my charge, my commandments, my statutes and my laws." Genesis 26:4-5

Faith and obedience go together. In fact, obedience to God is faith! It means you absolutely trust God, so you do what He tells you to do. I came to God when I was fourteen years old. I was a young girl who felt totally worthless. I was very immature. I felt the most important thing in life was to have a boyfriend. It would give me some worth. It was more than a desire; it was a need. There was like a huge hole inside me that even though I had God now I still had this need for a boyfriend. It was so strong it could have easily destroyed my life. In fact, there was a boy I liked at the time I got saved, and I knew he liked me too. The Lord told me, "No."

I obeyed. It wasn't easy because I had no balance whatsoever on the inside. As time went on, I liked other boys. The Lord would say, "No." I obeyed. We had a long, long list of no's before God finally said, "Yes."

My point is, giving God the place in your life to guide your decisions, and then obeying Him, IS FAITH. Suddenly this allusive thing called faith becomes very simple, it's obedience. When everything in you desires something, like in my case a boyfriend and you submit yourself to God's will for you. This is faith. And I learned to continue on this way into my adult life.

It is simple but it is hard. It is hard to obey the tiny voice of God in your heart when everything around may be shouting an opposite message to you. Like in my case my own emotions. Or sometimes it will be everyone around you, telling you the opposite. And you are hoping, somehow you haven't missed it, and you're really hearing God.

We see this throughout the Bible. By faith Noah obeyed God when God told him to build an ark. Even though at that time there was no rain on the earth, the earth was watered by mists. Noah dedicated his life to obeying the word of God, by building an ark. This was faith. I am sure the people around him thought he was crazy.

By faith Moses led the people out of Israel. He was a shepherd in the wilderness when God called him to go back to Egypt. Moses obeyed.

By faith Joshua marched around the walls of Jericho seven times and then blew a horn. This was not the usual way to win a battle. It all comes down to obedience.

Let's look at our verse in Genesis 26: 4-5. God says Abraham obeyed his voice. Not only did Abraham obey God's voice Abraham kept His charge, His laws, His statutes and His commandments. That is obedience in five different forms. This is truly a life of faith. Abraham obeyed God in every way possible. Like Abraham we need to do this.

What is His charge? For me in my life, I am a wife and mother, and now a grandmother. I take this very seriously. This is my responsibility to God. He has given me this charge and I do it. I never particularly liked cooking or housework, but I do it with joy. I am fulfilling my charge to God; I am caring for the family He has given me. I see my role as a wife and mother and as grandmother important work, because I have been charged by God to do this. I treat my husband the way God wants me to treat Him. The way I treat my husband has nothing to do with how my husband treats me; neither should your treatment of your mate depend on their behavior. It is your charge from God, and you will answer to Him. The same goes for your children. He doesn't have to tell me over and over to do this. It is up to me, and I obey Him in this way. Yes, this is faith.

What about His statutes, laws and commandments? First of all, we because of faith in God, we must obey His written word, not just His voice. Even among Christians this is rare. God does not have to tell you personally not to lie, not to steal, not to kill, not to commit sexual sins, like adultery, fornication, homosexuality, bestiality, etc... He has already told us this in His word. There is a lot in there to obey.

You may think, duh...we are Christians, we already know that. No, people don't know that. I have been a Christian a long time. I have been in churches that break God's laws without batting an eyelash. I visited one church, I was at their spaghetti supper. I overheard the pastor, who was eating his spaghetti next to me, congratulate the woman on the other side of me, for going to a Planned Parenthood rally in Washington.

I about fell off my chair! Christians promoting murder! You see it is easier to go with the popular thinking of our times than to obey the words written in the Bible.

It is true faith to change your life and your thinking and everything you know because the Bible tells you so. Those who do so have faith. I have seen those in the church committing adultery and claiming it was God's will. They think their situation makes them an exception to the rule. No, God does not have to tell you not to commit adultery; He has already said it in His word!

What about tithing? It is an act of faith. It takes your money, that you work so hard to earn, and raises it to a new level, the level of faith. It raises your trust, from the monetary system of the world, to the provision of God. You don't need a specific word from God to tithe, it is written in the Bible.

What about loving your enemies? Does God really expect you to do that? I know I couldn't, but I tried. There was someone I really hated in my life. I hated the man who broke up my parent's marriage. I tried and failed and tried and failed and tried and failed to forgive him and not hate him. Then God just took the hate away and it never came back.

Obedience to God's word IS faith. Do we want to follow the legacy of Abraham? Then we are to follow God's voice and His charge, also His commandments, His statutes and His laws. Even though it is not always popular, and even though our emotions may be screaming at us to do something else, and even though sometimes we are not even sure God is there, we obey. Yes, this is obedience, and this is faith.

Chapter Thirteen

Faith Comes by Hearing

So then faith comes by hearing, and hearing by the word of God. Romans 10:17

The word of God is essential when it comes to faith. If you're like me you and you desperately want more faith and you are saying to yourself, like I did, "So what does that verse mean? Does that mean, hearing someone preach the word of God. Or does that mean reading the word of God or speaking the word of God. Or does that mean when God speaks to you?" The answer is all of the above. They are all the word of God. Let's talk about all of them.

I want to talk about anointed preachers. A preacher has a little different anointing than a teacher. A preacher who is called by God, to preach the word of God, has anointing to bring faith to the hearers.

One of the greatest preachers of our time is Billy Graham. Billy Graham is a preacher; he has an anointing on his preaching for salvation. We are saved by faith. As Billy Graham preaches, those who hear, and I mean *hear*, remember Jesus was always saying that? Jesus was always saying, "Those with an ear let him hear." He was talking about listening with your heart, your inner man, your spirit. Those who *hear* as Billy preaches receive faith for salvation. It is such an awesome exciting thing to watch a Billy Graham crusade and see the altar call. The people come streaming to the altars. I have met many people through my years as a Christian, whom have been saved through Billy Graham's ministry. My sister Carol is one and she led me to the Lord.

God has many, many more anointed preachers than Billy Graham. I have two in my family. My son James has an anointing as a preacher. When he begins to preach, faith rises up within me. I can't wait to get to the altar to pray afterwards, because the faith rises as he preaches. He always says while he is preaching, "I am preaching to myself." And he gets excited and gets louder, and sometimes jumps a little bit. Something supernatural is happening.

My daughter Joy also has an anointing to preach. She has a heart for mission work and when she has been on the mission field she has preached. She told me about going to preach in the public schools in Ukraine she said, "Mom, the teenagers were just like teenagers here only maybe a little worse. The boys were so rebellious at school, sitting in class bored with an unlit cigarette in their mouths waiting for the bell to ring."

Joy was a teenager herself as she preached to the Ukrainian students. She told me their demeanor changed as she began to speak to them. She saw the cigarette drop out of one boy's mouth as he sat up to listen. The bell rang and not one student got up to leave. They were *hearing* the word of God for the first time, and something supernatural was happening in their hearts. Faith comes by hearing!!

One time I saw the angel that stands behind Joy as she preaches. This angel was picking up a signal from heaven and releasing it through Joy's preaching. Part of the angel's body had what reminded me of a UHF antenna that went from his shoulders up around his head. It was like one of those round, circle antennas, but in the entire circle was a swirl of transparent color. It reminded me of when you dip a bubble wand into a bottle of bubbles. That is what it was like in this circle, which was part of this angel that stands behind Joy as she preaches. It was beautiful. And I saw that as she preaches, and this angel stands behind her, with his hands on her shoulders. The angel was picking up a signal from heaven and somehow was transmitted through her preaching. Her preaching is supernatural; something powerful is released through this angel's antenna to the people listening. I wonder if many preachers have an angel like this, also? I don't know, but I do know anointed preaching causes faith to rise in the hearts of the hearers. People are saved; receive healing, deliverance or answers to prayer afterward because of the faith that rises as they listen. Faith comes by hearing and hearing by the word of God.

What about reading the Bible? Yes, the Bible is God's word and faith comes when we read it, to ourselves or to others. Many times, I have been reading the Bible when something jumps out at me, and I know God is speaking to me through it.

Another way faith comes from hearing is when God speaks to you directly. If God tells you something you can depend on it. The faith comes when He speaks, but a test will come also. Satan tries to steal God's word from our hearts. But we can hold onto that word, and it will come forth. Scripture tells us about this, in the parable of the sower.

"Behold a sower went out to sow. And as he sowed, some seed fell by the wayside; and the birds came and devoured them. Some fell on the stony places where they did not have much earth. But when the sun was up they were scorched, and because they had no root they withered away. And then some fell among thorns and the thorns sprang up and choked them. But others fell on good ground and yielded a crop: some a hundred-fold, some sixty, some thirty. He who has ears let him hear." Matthew13:3-9

Jesus explains later in the chapter that the seed is the word of God. *"Therefore, hear the parable of the sower: When anyone hears the word of the kingdom, and does not understand it, then the wicked one comes and snatches away what was sown in his heart. This is the seed by the wayside. But he who receives the seed on the stony places, this is he who hears the word and immediately receives it with joy; yet he has no root in himself but endures only for a while. For when tribulation or persecution arises because of the word, immediately he stumbles. Now he who received the seed among thorns is he, who hears the word, and the cares of this world and the deceitfulness of riches choke the word and he becomes unfruitful. But he who received the word on good ground is he who hears the word and understands it, who indeed bears fruit and produces; some a hundred-fold, some sixty, some thirty." Matthew 13:18-23*

Our hearts are the ground, in this parable, and God's word is the seed. When the conditions are right, and our hearts receive God's word correctly something wonderful happens. We produce a wonderful harvest. We receive faith and it grows, and we become fruitful in God's kingdom. I love it when this happens in my life!

But we see there are many things that can go wrong. We see the devil's activity in this parable. He does not want that seed to grow in your heart. In one part, this scripture tells us, he is snatching it from our hearts and in another place, it tells us persecutions will come BECAUSE OF The WORD! You can see we are going to have to hang on to produce fruit. Satan will oppose the word in our hearts.

Another part of our parable tells us the cares of the world and riches will choke out the word. This is my biggest problem, not the riches part but the cares part. We have to get rid of these so God's word in our hearts will produce faith and produce a crop.

Let this parable help you receive your harvest. When you feel God speaking His word to your heart, whether it is His voice, His word the Bible an anointed sermon, or any other of the many ways God speaks to us, {And there are MANY!}, be ready! Hold onto that word, don't let the blackbirds steal it, don't let the cares choke it, and don't let the persecution that is coming because of it cause you to release it. Hold onto it! Nurture it. Protect it! Cultivate it! Bear fruit! God's word will produce faith in our hearts and cause us to grow, produce and multiply.

God speaks to us on a daily basis if we will learn to listen. He can be very creative. Look for God to speak to you each day. He may speak to you through a friend, or a billboard, an animal, or something you see on television and of course he often speaks through dreams don't ignore them. I have even had God speak to me through a license plate and the numbers on a clock. Many, many times God has spoken to me through a book or a daily devotion.

One very special lady I know was sent encouragement from God by a ladybug. She had always collected lady bugs. She wore ladybug jewelry and had ladybug nick knacks all over her house. One time during a very trying experience a ladybug sat on her shoulder through the whole experience. It gave her courage and let her know she was not alone. It was not a coincidence.

Shut out the voices of the world and open yourself up to what God has to say. Listen to His voice. Read His word. He speaks to us daily. His daily word is available to us every single day. It is time to start listening. It is time to start really hearing with our real ears. It is time to start cultivating, growing and producing. Faith comes by HEARING!!!!

Chapter Fourteen
We Walk by Faith, Not by Sight

For we walk by faith and not by sight.
2 Corinthians 5:7

We live in the only realm that the reality of spiritual things is masked. We believe in a God we cannot see at this time, except through the eyes of our spirit. We believe in a world that is invisible to us. We follow a tiny voice inside us, the voice of the Holy Spirit, which is so quiet it can easily be dismissed. We believe the world is full of angels and demons even though we cannot see them. We believe our loved ones who have gone before us, still exist in heaven and we will see them again. We believe in the unseen. They can see us, but we can't see them.

Many people think we are crazy. They only believe in what they can see. Mankind has made up silly ridiculous theories of how we came to exist, which are harder to believe than to believe in God.

I remember in high school and these theories being taught as fact. In my biology class I was getting straight A's until it came to evolution. Back then evolution was thought by most to be true. I remember thinking, I don't care if every bit of evidence in the world proves otherwise, I know the Bible is true! I believe in the story of creation in Genesis 1. I didn't even listen when the teacher taught otherwise and when it came time for the test at the end of the session, I did not answer one question. I wrote on the front of the test…. "In the beginning God created the heavens and the earth." Of course, I got a zero on the test. I didn't care.

Since then, it has come out that most of the evidence for evolution was false and now even unbelieving scientists are proving what the Bible has told us all along. Whether science proves it or not I don't care.

God made the decision that mankind would have to walk by faith and not by sight for a reason. He knows best. But this is only temporary and even on earth this will come to an end. Jesus will soon return to earth and every eye shall see Him.

There is a great blessing for those who believe what they have not seen. We see this matter in the gospel of John, in chapter 20. Jesus has been crucified and has risen from the dead but Thomas, like many today, refused to believe. Let's read it.

But Thomas, called Didymus, one of the twelve, was not with them when Jesus came. The other disciples therefore said to him, "We have seen the Lord." But he said to them, "Unless I see His hands the print of the nails and put my finger into the print of the nails, and put my hand into His side, I will not believe." And again, after eight days His disciples were again inside and Thomas was with them. Jesus came the doors being shut, and stood in the midst, and said, "Peace to you!"

Then He said to Thomas, "Reach your finger here, and look at my hands; and reach your hand here and put it into My side. Do not be unbelieving but believing."

And Thomas answered and said, "My Lord and my God!"

Jesus said to him, "Thomas, because you have seen Me, you have believed. Blessed are those who have not seen and yet have believed." John 20:24-29

Jesus spoke of a blessing on those who believe and yet they haven't seen. I want to tell you a story of one such woman.

I want to tell you of a story of a woman who lived in communist Russia during the cold war. Christians were persecuted and put in prisons and mental institutions. This woman I will call her Dalia she wasn't a Christian because she didn't know God. She was not sure if Christianity was true or if God was real. But she thought it might be true. She realized that if it was true, then her government was wrong. Because of her thought that God might be real, she refused to join the communist party. Her husband didn't understand but he loved her. She was pressured to join the communist party, but she couldn't, just because she thought God might be real. She refused on that chance. She was put in a mental institution and tortured. While she was there her mind snapped and she agreed to whatever they wanted. But soon her mind returned, and she realized that she couldn't join the communist party. Even though she knew she was going to suffer terribly, she again refused the communists. She just couldn't let go of that chance that it might all be true, that God might be real, and if He was nothing could be more important. This woman had faith. She was willing to suffer just for the hope that God was real.

You see, faith is so much more than just getting things from God. Faith is holding onto God and never letting go. Faith is reaching into the unseen. Faith is living a life that no one else understands just because you want to please Him. Dalia's life did please Him. Very few would pay so great a price for just a hope. What Dalia did is awesome! Dalia put such a high price on God that just for the hope of Him, which she could not see; she gave up the life that she could see. Great is her reward!

God has chosen that those of us on earth must walk by faith and not by sight. We don't see His magnificent glory as the angels do, and they fall down on their faces in utter worship and adoration. I would like to quote for you a passage from one of my favorite books, *The Call,* by Rick Joyner. In this portion of the book Rick, the author, is in a vision and talking to Jesus.

"My father has entrusted Me with all power. I can command the heavens and they obey me, but I cannot command love. Love commanded is not love at all. There will be a time when I demand obedience from the nations, but then the time to prove your love will have passed. While I am not demanding obedience,

those who come to Me obey Me because they love Me and love the truth. These are the ones who will be worthy to reign with Me in My kingdom, those who love Me and serve me in spite of persecution and rejection. You must want to come to Me. Those who become Our dwelling place will not come because of a command, or just because they know My power—they will come because they love Me and they love the Father.

"Those who come to the truth will come because they love Us. It is because of the darkness that this is the age of true love. True love shines the brightest against the greatest darkness. You love Me more when you see Me with the eyes of your heart and obey Me, even though your eyes cannot see Me as they do now. Love and worship will be the greatest in the great darkness that is coming upon the earth. Then all of creation will know that your love for Me is true and why We desire to dwell with men.

"Those who come to Me now, fighting through all the forces of the world that rebel against me, come because they have the true love of God. They want to be with Me so much that even when it all seems so unreal, even when I seem like a vague dream to them, they will risk all for the hope the dream is real. That is love. That is the love of the truth. <u>That is the faith that pleases My Father.</u> All will bow the knee to Me when they see My power and glory, but those who bow the knee now when they can only see me dimly through the eyes of faith are the obedient ones who love Me in Spirit and in truth. These I will soon entrust with the power and the glory of the age to come, which is stronger than any

darkness."

There is a reason we must walk by faith and not by sight. It has to do with the high calling we are called to. The power and glory of the age to come will be trusted to those who believe this way.

I underlined the sentence on faith. I don't just want you, my readers, to have faith; I want you to have the kind of faith that pleases the Father. The faith like Abraham had. That leaves all, obeys all and sacrifices all, for God, the unseen, who will be your eternal dwelling place. And one day this veil will be lifted, and you will see Him. But until then we walk by faith and not by sight

Chapter Fifteen

Faith Works by Love

The only thing that counts is faith expressing itself through love. Ephesians 5:6b {NIV}.

There is a huge connection between faith and love. This verse tells us that faith is expressed through love. Faith and love go hand in hand. Love is the power behind faith. Faith activates God; God is love. We are told in scripture that God is love. *He who does not love does not know God, for God is love. 1 John 4:8.* We are not told in this verse that God has love, but that God is love. There is nothing stronger than God and there is nothing stronger than love.

Let us keep looking at this. God has expressed His great love toward us, through Jesus. We on this planet, since the fall of Adam, had been doomed. God in His great love expressed His love, in human form, that was Jesus. Jesus, we know in the eternal form was called the Word.

[John 1} He, the eternal deity called the Word, was sent by the Father, through love, and came to earth in human form. He is no longer called the Word. He has eternally changed to become our Savior; He is now the Son of God. This is not a one-time act, but an eternal position that He now takes on. He is eternally now the Son of God, our High Priest, He is the first born of many, we being the many.

Let us look at this yet again, deeper this time. We were without hope. We were eternal beings, from a fallen race that were eternally lost. The angels that had fallen were lost, also, but there is no repentance for them, it is not possible. Now mankind has fallen also, there was no way for us. We were doomed to the same eternity as Satan, the deceiver who deceived Adam and Eve, our grandparents. We inherited sin and a sin nature. There was no way for us ……. until, Jesus became our Way.

Jesus told us, "I am the Way; no one comes to the Father except through Me." He did not make a way for us; He became our Way. There was no other way, the cost was huge, but Jesus came to earth and became our Way of salvation. The love behind this is incomprehensible! It is beyond our ability to imagine! God coming to earth and becoming flesh.

Jesus did not just take thirty-three years out of his eternal life to come and save us. No! He has eternally changed forms; He has entered earth, not in the form of God but as a baby. He has come to Earth as the Son of Man. He comes on a mission, to save us. He lays down His life for us. He now is eternally our Savior, our High Priest, and the Son of God. There was no way, and He became the Way, by becoming like us, by coming here and taking on our sin, defeating hell and the grave. Jesus did not make a way, He became the Way, and now through Him, we have a Way. The only, only, only, only Way is Jesus. Jesus has eternally laid down his eternal life for us to become the Way for us.

LOVE, LOVE, LOVE, LOVE, UNIMAGINABLE LOVE. Through faith in Him. {think sumo Jesus' suit} we are saved. We partake of His flesh, we partake of His blood, and we are IN HIM, forever. The love Jesus displayed toward us and the magnitude of what He did for us, and understanding it, the best that we can, is a secret to faith. Faith and love work together.

Now through faith in Jesus, we have the opportunity to respond to that love. Jesus out of love came to earth and operated in faith. Now we have an opportunity through faith IN HIM to respond back to Him and walk in love, in faith, with Him. Everything Jesus did on earth was faith working through love. And now we respond the same way, by faith into a love relationship with God, love and faith working together. God operates in faith through love and so must we.

Not only was Jesus coming to earth motivated by love, when Jesus walked the earth, He performed miracles by faith that was expressed through love. Let's look in the gospel at some of His miracles.

And when Jesus went out, He saw a great multitude; and He was moved with compassion for them and healed their sick. Matthew 14:14

*Then a leper came to Him, imploring Him, kneeling
down to Him and saying to Him, "If You are willing, you
can make me clean." And <u>Jesus moved with compassion</u>,
put out His hand and touched him, and said to him, "I am
willing: be though cleansed." Mark 1:40-41*

*Now it happened the day after that He went into a
city called Nain; and many of his disciples went with Him,
and a large crowd. And when He came near the gate of the
city, behold a dead man was being carried out, the only
son of a mother; and she was a widow. And a large crowd
from the city was with her. When the Lord saw her, <u>He had
compassion on her</u> and said to her, "Do not weep." Then
He came and touched the coffin, and those who carried
him stood still. And He said, "Young man, I say to you
arise." And he who was dead sat up and began to speak.
And He presented him to his mother. Luke 7:11-15*

Here we see faith working through love. The
miracles of Jesus are love in action brought about by faith.
By faith in the love of God, we receive what the love of
God has provided for us, by faith. Jesus operated in faith
motivated by love, and we are to operate the same way,
faith in His love.

*Therefore, be followers of God as dear Children.
And walk in love, as Christ also has loved us and given
Himself for us, an offering and a sacrifice to God as a
sweet-smelling aroma. Ephesians 5:1-2*

The greatest act of love and faith, ever, was God's

faith and love toward us on the cross. It is the great mystery. The power of it is unfathomable. Remember love is the greatest power in the universe. Now remember the greatest act of love, ever is Jesus on the cross; God in the form of flesh laying down His eternal life to become our Savior.

It is hard to see in our world. The smoke and smog of the kingdom of darkness, that cloud of depression and sin covering our planet by its ruler the prince of the power of the air who seeks to blind the minds of men from the truth of gospel, makes this glorious mystery hard to see.{Ephesians 2:1-3}

But it is there, and with eyes of faith we need gaze upon it. Its beauty and depths are beyond our ability to fathom in this lifetime. Its power is unimaginable. Those in the eternal realm are awed by it and long to understand it. The patriarchs and prophets glimpsed it in the future and longed for it. The angels desire to look into it.

Of this salvation the prophets have inquired and searched diligently, who prophesied of the grace that would come to you, searching what, or what manner of time, the Spirit of Christ who was in them was indicating when He testified beforehand the sufferings of Christ and the glories that would follow. To them it was revealed that not to themselves, but to us, they were ministering the things which now have been reported to you through those who have preached the gospel to you by the Holy Spirit sent down from heaven—things which angels desire to look into.1 Peter 1:10-12

The secret of the ages, God's plan of salvation for

man revealed, the cross. Our faith and love were birthed, through Christ's act of faith and love toward us. It is the birth of our faith and the strength of our faith. Jesus Christ is the author and finisher of our faith. To gaze and dwell and feed on this Great Mystery of love working through faith will transform us.

I love testimonies. I have read as many as I can get my hands on. I've read stories of those whose lives were transformed from unbelievable darkness, sin and hopelessness, in an instant, by the power of the gospel. In a moment of time, hardened criminals are forever changed. They are changed to those who spread the good they have received from God, for the remainder of their lives, just by coming in contact with this, mystery, this unbelievable act of love, of God, for mankind, you.

I have read of inmates in prison hopelessly lost, coming to the Lord in an instant and then dedicating their life to a ministry to prisons. They go back to the place that seemed like hell to them to offer hope to others. It is the power of the gospel.

In our town of Lakeland, there was a boy's home started by an ex-heroin addict who had come to Jesus. He was helping boys that had no hope, just like he once had no hope. The power of the gospel! And there is more I have read of hardened men from motorcycle gangs becoming preachers, prostitutes coming to Jesus and serving Him, witch doctors and those from the occult, alcoholic's and gangsters all changed in an instant, by the power of the gospel, and then dedicating their lives to God, and then doing the works Jesus did.

It has happened to me; in one instant I went from darkness to light. I instantly became a new person. That is the power of the gospel. There are millions of such testimonies, yours too. Everyone's testimony is different, and everyone's beautiful.

We have come face to face with the greatest act of love ever and it has forever changed us. The faith of God working by love was Jesus becoming the Way for us so that now we can also through faith and love continue His work on earth. We can join with Him and move with Him in His faith and love to those around us, and become a part, in this eternal story, which is now being written for all of eternity. The story of Christ continues through us. It is written by faith working by love.

I want to end this chapter by quoting a passage from the book, *The Final Quest,* by Rick Joyner. In this passage Rick is in a conversation with Jesus on this very subject. Jesus is the speaker, and He is telling Rick about faith working by love.

"Before the end, I must reveal My power on earth. Even so, the greatest power that I have ever revealed on earth, or ever will, is still a very small demonstration of My power. I do not reveal My power to get men to believe in My power, but to get men to believe in My love. If I had wanted to save the world with My power when I walked the earth, I could have moved mountains by pointing a finger. Then all men would have bowed to Me, but not because they loved Me, or loved the truth, but because they feared My power. I do not want men to obey Me because they fear My power, but because they love Me,

and they love the truth.

"If you do not know My love, then My power will corrupt you. I do not give you love so that you can know My power, but I give you My power so that you can know My love. The goal of your life must be love, not power. Then I will give you power to love with. I will give you power to heal the sick because you love them, and I love them, and I do not want them sick.

"So, you must seek love first, and then faith. You cannot please Me without faith. But faith is not just the knowledge of My power but the knowledge of My love and the power of My love. Faith must first be for love. Seek faith to love more and do more with your love. Only when you seek faith to love can I trust you with My power. Faith works by love."

Chapter Sixteen

The Power of Faith

"For assuredly, I say to you, if you have faith as a mustard seed, you will say to this mountain, 'Move from here to there,' and it will move; and nothing will be impossible for you." Matthew 17:20

Years ago I read a book called, *Miracle in the Mirror,* about a young girl named, Nita Edwards. Nita was injured in an accident falling down the stairs. She became totally paralyzed. She had one complication after another until there was no more hope for her and the doctors gave her up to die. The paralysis even crept up her throat and she could only eat liquids. She shrunk down to eighty pounds. Her last request was to leave the hospital. She wanted to get an apartment and be cared for there by her caregivers. Even against the doctors' orders her friends and family removed her frail, paralyzed body from the hospital. This was around Christmas time in 1976. Of course, many people had prayed for her healing, but it seemed to no avail.

As Nita was lying on her death bed, she thought she heard a voice from someone in the room, "I am going to heal you on February 11," the voice said. When she realized there was no one in the room, she came to believe that God had spoken to her.

"God if that is you," she prayed, "please give me some confirmation."

Later a visitor that came to see her gave her a word from God, "God is going to send you as a messenger to Asia."

Nita took that as confirmation the voice was from God. Next, she prayed, God, you've given me the day, now give me the time."

"Three thirty," she heard. Now she began anticipating her healing on that day.

As I was reading this book, I started thinking to myself, "Oh no, she is going to be so disappointed, when nothing happens on that day."

It just seemed too big of a miracle. I had been in many healing meetings, but I had never seen a quadriplegic get out of a wheelchair.

As February 11, 1977, came, Nita had invited people to her apartment, because she wanted them to witness her miracle. Her mother, some friends, and her caregiver were all there. They spent the time in prayer. Three o'clock came, and then three twenty, Nita was fervently in prayer.

I held my breath as I continued reading. I wondered; would she really be healed?

At three thirty her bed began to shake, as Jesus, in a blinding light, entered her room, she long to reach out and touch him. The next thing she knew she was catapulted from her bed, and she landed on the floor at the foot of her bed on her knees.

I gasped as I read this.

Her mother who had felt the bed began to shake opened her eyes from prayer, just in time to see her daughter's withered hand straighten and then see her catapult from the bed. Nita rose from the floor and walked, even though all the muscles had atrophied away. Nita was totally healed! She has since become a missionary to Asia and has a ministry called Asia Alive.

I don't what my problem was, why I thought something would be too hard for God? The power of faith is the power to heal any disease, any sickness, no matter how severe. Nothing is too hard for God.

We used to have a healing room in the church I attended. The people praying in it had been trained by Charles and Frances Hunter's Healing School. The healing rooms were open for prayer before service and immediately afterward. We used to linger after services and worship for twenty minutes or so. One day a man came running out of the healing room screaming and yelling and jumping around. When the ushers finally calmed him down, he told us all that he had just been healed. He was blind and when he was prayed for, and now, he suddenly could see, that's when he ran out yelling, he was just so happy!

The power of faith is more than enough power to heal any disease or to create new eyeballs, or ear drums or whatever body part that is needed.

But there is more. God has millions of angels at His command. The Bibles tells us there are armies of angels at His command. Our faith in God will dispatch His angels on our behalf.

I will never forget my first winter driving when I was sixteen years old. My dad provided my sister and I, an old relic to drive. It was a 1963, Ford Galaxy, it had been my great grandfather's before he died. It had seen better days and the tires were no better, they were bald.

On Christmas Eve, that year, instead of going to church with my parents and sister, I went to a friend's house, in the old Galaxy. When I left and began to drive home that night, the weather had gotten very bad, and the roads were very icy. I came to the first stop sign and tried to stop, and I slid right through.

"Oh, no," I thought to myself, "I can't make it home in this car." We lived quite a way out of town on a lake. I decided to drive to the church and catch up with my parents and drive home with them, church was in town.

I was too late, when I got to the church, my parents were already gone. The roads were continually getting icier, and I was terrified. I started for home, but I didn't get far. The first little hill I got to, I could see a line of cars, all the way up. They couldn't make it; it was too icy. There were about five cars ahead of me that were not moving. I didn't even get close to where they were, and they had much better cars than I, but they were all sliding and unable to climb the little hill. At the base of the hill my tires started to spin, and my car stopped moving. I stepped on the gas, but the tires just whirred around, and I was stuck.

I was terrified. There were no houses around and even if there were, I wouldn't have dared to go to one. I was still many miles from home; it was too far and too cold to walk. It was Christmas Eve and I wanted to go HOME! I prayed. I said, "God, would you send your angels to push my car home."

Suddenly my car started moving forward. My tires were still spinning but my car was moving forward about five or ten miles an hour. I felt like I was being pushed. I started moving up the hill and then I got to where the other cars were stuck. I was still moving so I got in the oncoming lane and slowly passed every car. Even though I could hear the tires spinning, my car was still moving forward at a steady rate of speed. I passed every stuck car and continued on. That was the small hill. The big hill was coming. Green Hill, we called it. It was the only way home; it was a steep hill, the worst hill around. I would have to get up that one before I got home. The same thing happened. I got to that hill and there was a long line of cars not moving. My tires spun all the way up, but my little old car kept a steady speed and passed them all. When I made it home my family were all waiting for me, wondering if I would make it. I ran in and told them how angels pushed me all the way home!

The power of faith has the power of myriads of

angels behind it, the power of faith dispatches powerful angels to come to our aid! But that is not all, there is more. The power of faith can transcend natural laws of nature. Using faith Jesus calmed the storm and walked on water.

For Moses, the Red Sea parted, and water came flowing from rocks. And for Joshua, the huge walls of Jericho came crashing down and the sun even stood still. Shadrach, Meshach and Abednego were not burned in a furnace that was so hot that the guards that threw them in the fire were immediately burned up.

Miracles like these do still happen today. In his book, *Like a Mighty Wind*, Mel Tari talks about a revival that came to his church, in a little village called Timor, in Indonesia. From his church the Lord led these people to take the message of the Gospel to other villages in the jungle. The teams that went through the jungle saw many miracles. God would lead them through the jungle with a bright light at night. Mel said it was as bright as the lights at the airport; it would lead them through the jungle. They also crossed a flooded river by walking on the water, prayed over water for communion that turned to wine, and even a cloud would come over them by day to shield them from the sun as they traveled through the jungle. They would encounter witch doctors and many others who would try to use their magic to stop them to no avail. At one village the people poisoned their food. The little band of weary Christian travelers being hungry unwittingly ate the poisoned food and then began to preach. The people of the village waited for them to fall down and die, but the poison never affected them. The village people were amazed and listened to their message.

Yes, the power of faith can transcend natural human laws. What else can the power of faith do? It also had an effect on animals. Remember, in the Bible, when Daniel was thrown into the lion's den. The lions never touched him.   The next day when Daniel's enemies were thrown in, they were immediately devoured. The power of faith can stop an animal attack.

My dad encountered this. When I was in high school, my dad worked at a bank as the collection's manager. My dad would have to repossess people's cars if they stopped paying for them. My dad is a kind person and would give people the opportunity to work things out but there were times that he would have to repossess things. This could be dangerous; people would try many things.

One day my dad and another man from the bank went to pick up a car. These people were determined to keep their car by force and sent a ferocious dog out to stop them. The dog came charging out, and my dad's coworker, who came with dad from the bank, was scared and jumped behind my dad. God had been dealing with dad prior to this about our restoration in Christ. That just as Adam had authority over animals, so did we because that was restored to us in Christ. As this ferocious dog jumped at my dad's throat, my dad thought of this, and he stood up and faced the dog in faith. He said in midair that the attacking dog just fell to his feet, whimpering. The people came out of their house amazed; they kept saying over and over we never saw our dog act like that before. It sat at my dad's feet. The people, somewhat in awe of my dad, didn't put up any more fight and turned over the key to their car. The power of faith can stop an animal attack.

But the power of faith can do even more than that. It can make something out of nothing! The Bible tells us in Hebrews 11:3 *By faith we understand that the worlds were framed by the word of God, so that the things which are seen are not made of things which are visible.*

God created the world through faith, His own faith. Faith has the power to create something from nothing. This can really blow our minds.

I remember a very touching story I read in the Guidepost magazine one time. It was written by a woman whose husband was scheduled to have heart surgery. The day before the surgery, the two of them set out to have a memorable day together. They stopped their car and decided to go for a little walk. They followed a trail through a dusty arid area and found the most beautiful spot. It was lush and green and there was a beautiful pool of water. The spot was so refreshing that they sat on a rock by the pool and spent the afternoon there, just enjoying each other's company and the beautiful spot they found.

Later, when they got back to the car, her husband told her, "I left my pocketknife back there on the rock, we sat on." She told her husband to wait there in the car and she would go back and get his knife. She followed the trail back, but there was no pool of water. She located the rock, and the knife was still there, but the beautiful spot was no longer green and the pool where they had spent the afternoon was gone. It was nothing but dry desert. She gasped in shock. She returned to the car and her husband.

The next day, during the heart surgery, her husband died. She realized that God had given her a beautiful afternoon, to remember with her husband. In His great love, He had created a spot for them to enjoy. That is the heart of our wonderful God. But you see it is nothing for Him to create something, from nothing.

The power of faith is limitless because it is God's power. Faith is the vehicle that we use to receive from God. And what we can receive from God is beyond imagination, because it is His power that we tap into, when we use faith. Jesus told us if we have faith as big as a mustard seed, we can move a mountain. Faith has power. Faith has very great power. Look around you, faith is behind everything you see. It goes as high as the stars and as deep as the ocean. God has infinite power and everything He does is good. Faith avails us to all He has for us. That is what makes faith so powerful.

Chapter Seventeen

Stepping Out in Faith

And in the fourth watch of the night Jesus went to them walking on the sea. And when the disciples saw Him walking on the sea, they were troubled saying, "It is a ghost!" And they cried out in fear. But immediately Jesus spoke to them, saying, "Be of good cheer! It is I; do not be afraid." And Peter answered Him saying, "Lord if it is you, and command me to come to you on the water." And He said, "Come." And when Peter had come down out of the boat, he walked on the water to go to Jesus. Matthew 14:25-29

For a few minutes Peter was able to walk on top of the water. I have to admire Peter; he was the only disciple who even tried to walk on the water. He was the only disciple who stepped out of the boat and tried. Something amazing happens when people step out in faith. Like Peter we will find out that miracles really can happen. I want to talk about stepping out in faith.

All three of my children stepped out in faith and went to Bible Schools. My son is the oldest and he went first. It was such a huge stretch of the imagination that my son would ever go to college that I never even dared dream of it. The thought never even entered my head. Not only was it financially impossible it was just plain impossible. My son has learning disabilities and the only grade he had ever passed was kindergarten. I didn't even think there was hope that he would get a high school education, let alone college.

He stepped out in faith. He managed to get a G.E.D. and working at a fast-food restaurant he saved up for a used car. Then my teen-aged son with no help from his financially struggling parents left home and traveled 800 miles away to a Bible College. His learning disabilities had been so difficult I didn't think he could do it, but he did. It was tough but he did it. He supported himself doing telephone sales. He walked into a large telephone sales office and within the first month he was their top seller. He struggled with his schoolwork but by his senior year my son made the dean's list. He stepped out in faith and did the impossible.

Next was my daughter Joy. She was only seventeen when she trekked out to her Bible school. She also left home in an old used car she had saved up for. I couldn't stand the thought of her driving so far alone, so I drove with her and took a bus home. She was going to Morning Star School in South Carolina. When I took her there, she had very little money and needed a job right away. I also had very little money, but I bought her a blow-up bed to sleep in and some bread and bologna. It was all I could do. The night before I was to take the bus home, I lay awake wondering how I could leave my little girl in a strange city so far away to fend for herself. I wanted to just bring her home, I was so troubled.

In the middle of the night, I felt a powerful presence come in the room. It was an angel and somehow, he communicated with me. He told me he had been with Paul in the book of Acts during his shipwreck. He told me every person on the ship was saved, they were saved by angels. He let me know that just as he saw to it that each soul on the ship was saved, he would see to it, in the same way, that each of my daughter's needs would be met. This angel had come to help her. Joy stepped out in faith, her year was difficult, but she made it.

My daughter Lonna also went to Morning Star School two years later. All three of my children stepped out in faith and went to Bible School. I want to tell you about some of the adventures Joy and Lonna went through at their school, an amazing school that actually teaches how-to walk-in faith. It was called their faith course and they would receive faith assignments. When they would call home and tell me about their faith assignments, I felt like I was listening to the book of Acts. As they stepped out in faith, God would meet them time and time again. Their faith assignments are the motivation for this chapter.

One of Joy's faith assignments was to go to the mall and pray for someone that the Lord would lead her to. As Joy was walking around the mall praying, she felt drawn to a certain man. She walked back to pray for him, but he was gone. Later that day she saw him again. "Weren't you at the mall earlier?" she asked him.

"Yes," the man replied.

"I have been looking for you to pray for you," Joy told him. "I felt God leading me to you to pray for you," she added.

The man began to cry. "I was sitting there in the mall asking God to send me someone to pray with me," the man said through tears. "My wife is sick in the hospital."

Joy prayed with the man, and he left rejoicing. Things like that were daily occurrences in the faith course. One of their assignments was to receive a phone number from God and call it and give the person that answered a word from God. Joy's roommate called the number God gave her and gave the man at the other end the word God had for him. He was amazed. She had called a professional football player whose phone number was unlisted. After talking with him, he decided to start going back to church.

Another girl in the class received her phone number to call in a dream. She woke up and although she was nervous, she stepped out in faith and called the number from her dream. She was given a simple message to tell who answered, just that God loved the person, and He was thinking about them. She had no idea where she was calling but she nervously stepped out in faith; she called the number and a woman answered.

"I got your number from God," she told the woman

on the line, her voice trembling, "and He wanted me to tell you He is thinking about you, and He loves you."

"That is the craziest thing I ever heard in my life!" She heard the woman exclaim.

The young girl thought of hanging up, but she hung on. The woman paused and then added, "Last night, before I went to bed I prayed and told God, 'If your real then let me know somehow.' Now the first thing this morning you call and tell me God gave you my phone number and to call and tell me He loves me!" She paused again and then added, "I think I want to serve Him."

The student prayed with the women to be saved, but that wasn't all. This woman was raising her younger brother and sister because their parents had died and soon, they came in the room. When their sister told them what had just happened, they too wanted to pray. Just as they were finished praying this woman's fiancé came in, when he heard the story, he also prayed. Before the faith student had hung up the phone, all were saved and all four of them had filled the bathtub and baptized each other and all four were speaking in tongues!!!!!

I couldn't wait to hear from my daughters when they were in school. Their faith assignments were amazing. Sometimes they would have to bring supplies to a homeless person. God would lead them to just the right person. Sometimes the power of God would fall, right on the street and a crowd would gather as the students would tell them the gospel and pray, on the sidewalks.

Then it was time for Joy's final exam. Four girls were assigned together. They were given a certain city in a southern state to go to. They were to go without money; they had to go by faith. They had a list of things they had to accomplish while they were there. They had to find a place to stay, eat, and do everything by faith. They had to put on a meeting in a public place, and they also had to put on a meeting at a church. They had to get their meals by faith. They had to get a meeting with the chief of police of the town and give him a word from God, a skill they learned in school. There were many things they had to accomplish; they even had to sing karaoke at a restaurant.

Off the girls went. They found a hotel that let them stay for free. They found a church that let them come in and have a meeting. They ministered and gave the people their prophetic words {part of their training} and everyone there was blessed. They had their meeting in the park and ministered to homeless people. Each task they were assigned had amazing results. Strangers were ministered to; people's lives were touched. They continued on with their assigned list. But when they tried to contact the chief of police they were refused by the chief's staff. It looked like that would not get accomplished. They were also getting hungry.

Although they had no money for food, they went in a place that had karaoke and started singing because that was on their list. As they were singing, in walked the chief of police. They approached him; they told them had tried to see him earlier to give him a word from God. They spoke the word God gave them to give him and he broke down in tears. He insisted on buying their lunch. Everything they had set out to do by faith they accomplished.

I was amazed when I heard the stories. I wondered if we all asked God to use us and began to step out in faith if this could be an everyday experience for all of us. My daughter Lonna has had similar experiences while she was at school and since she has been out of school as well. Sometimes she does stuff I can't believe. She has God adventures. One time she felt God was giving her a message for a famous entertainer. She wrote the message down; it was several pages long and put them in an envelope. She wondered how she would give it to him. Well Lonna's aunt who has an airline job brought her with her to Las Vegas. {If you're really religious you won't like this story} This entertainer happened to be starring in Las Vegas, but it still looked impossible. The seats at the front of the auditorium cost thousands of dollars. Lonna was way in the back and there were guards everywhere keeping people back. She decided to try. Even though the guards were not letting anyone through to the front, Lonna started walking forward and no one stopped her. She kept going climbing over barriers until she was in front of the stage. The famous entertainer then actually bent down and pulled Lonna up on the stage to dance. She danced around to his back pocket and slipped the letter in it. He looked confused and asked her what it was, she told him a letter and left. She had done her part she had stepped out in faith and delivered the message the rest was up to God. Lonna has these adventures because she steps out in faith.

I love the book of Acts. The disciples began

stepping out in faith, preaching the gospel, healing the sick, boldly facing their opposers. Every day was a new adventure in faith, just as my children did in school, every day a new adventure of stepping out and believing God.

I have stepped out in faith from time to time in my life, but I wonder if this could be a daily adventure. Perhaps if I were to, on a daily basis, to step out of my own little boat, my comfort zone, and step out onto the sea, maybe I would begin to see miracles daily too; maybe I could walk on water.

VolumeFive

The Hall of Faith

Chapter Eighteen

So What Is Faith?

Through the years I have gained some
understanding on faith. I know I still have a long way to go.
I used to think in order to strum up faith I would have to
work myself up to a Pentecostal frenzy. That faith was
getting your head convinced that something was going to
happen. I wanted something concrete, something I could
hold. I knew faith was the key to getting my prayers
answered. And to some degree it wasn't my fault I felt this
way. I would go to revival meetings and the leader of the
meeting would have to get us pumped up. We would sing
a bunch of worship songs, until the mood was right. And as
the leader up front would be praying for the sick, he'd
holler, "Don't stop worshipping! Don't stop praying!"

Somehow if we stopped it would kill the mood and the faith would go out the window. And really there is some truth to this. Worship gets our eyes on God. But faith isn't an emotion we have to strum up.

One time, years ago, my husband and I went to a healing meeting. It was different than all the meetings I had been in before. It was a Charles and Frances Hunter meeting. Maybe you younger folks have never heard of them, but to those of us, who have been around Christianity for a while, we know that their meetings were tremendous. In this meeting Charles stood up and said that they were going to pray for the sick in faith. He told us we didn't need any songs or any hype that the Bible gave us authority to heal the sick and they were going to use that authority. He said that he and Frances had a special faith for back pain and slipped discs. So, he asked if anyone in the audience had such a problem. Several people came up.

The first one was a young man about thirty. Charles interviewed him. He held the microphone up to him and asked the man what the problem was. We learned this young man had an injury and was in constant pain. You could see the pain on his face, and even the way he was dressed. He was wearing loose sweatpants. You could even hear the pain in his voice. He could no longer work and was scheduled for surgery. He was hoping it would help him enough that he could get back to work. Then Charles checked his mobility to see what he could do. The man could barely move he was in so much pain. Bending over was out of the question.

"Well, you are not going to need the surgery," Charles told the man, "Because God is going to do surgery on you." Then Charles turned to us, the audience and said I am simply going to pray for him, no tricks and he is going to be healed."

I had been in so many healing meetings and yes, people had gotten healed, but this was so different. There wasn't any big build-up, just a simple explanation. The prayer took all of thirty seconds. Charles actually commanded the man's back to be healed. He commanded the discs to be healed and then he said, "It's done." Then he said to the man, "Now begin to move, do what you couldn't do before."

The man began to move. He moved some more. I will as long as I live never forget the look on this man's face as he suddenly realized he was completely healed. It brings tears to my eyes to think of it. He suddenly realized he could bend over and move, and he was in no pain. He looked at his wife who was standing nearby, he couldn't speak because he was so overcome with emotion. His eyes said it all. It was a beautiful moment. And then he began to cry because he realized his terrible ordeal was over.

This changed my perception of faith. It wasn't something allusive that had to be conjured up. It was in hand, and it was real. I was in awe.

Faith is not a feeling. It is not an emotion. It is invisible but it is real. I believe true faith is a tenacious belief in the goodness of God, a knowing and believing that His word is true. Faith looks past the seen to the unseen. It sees a God that is greater than any problem and knows that He cares. Faith is always in God and His capability, not in ourselves. It will hang on if need be. It will never let go.

There have been times I have received from God by faith because I have done what God has told me to do and I obeyed. But that doesn't mean my emotions were on board. I have felt very small and wondered is this really God or am I crazy?!! Faith is not a feeling.

Faith has substance. Faith obeys God, it is obedience, no matter what. Faith hangs onto the belief that God is good, no matter what happens and no matter what it seems like at the time. Faith will risk everything. Faith will keep you hanging on when everyone is telling you to let go. Faith sees farther than life on this earth. Faith looks far ahead into eternity and causes you to live differently. Faith is putting your hand to the plow and never quitting. It is never turning back, even if there is a cross and a tomb in front of you. It moves you forward past the tomb, to the resurrection. Faith is knowing that God is good, His word is always true, and you can always trust Him. And most of all true faith is always, always in God, knowing that we can come before for Him, in right standing. Because our marvelous Savior has made us clean before Him. Faith is understanding what Christ has done for you, and what is now yours, bought and paid for by the blood of the Savior.

Chapter Nineteen

The Hall of Faith

Now Faith is the substance of things hoped for, the evidence of things not seen. For by it the elders obtained a good testimony. By faith we understand that the worlds were framed by the word of God, so that the things which are seen were not made of things which are visible. By faith Abel offered to God a more excellent sacrifice than Cain, through which he obtained witness that he was righteous, God testifying of his gifts; and through it he being dead still speaks. By faith Enoch was translated so that he did not see death, "and was not found because God had translated him"; for before his translation he had this testimony, that he pleased God. But without faith it is impossible to please Him, for he who comes to God must believe that He is and that He is a rewarder of those who diligently seek Him. By faith Noah, being divinely warned of things not yet seen, moved with godly fear, prepared an ark for the saving of his household, by which he condemned the world and became heir of the righteousness which is according to faith. By faith Abraham obeyed when he was called to go out to the place he would afterward receive as an inheritance. And he went out, not knowing where he was going. By faith he sojourned in the land of promise as in a foreign country, dwelling in tents with Isaac and Jacob, the heirs with him of the same promise; for he waited for the city that has foundations, whose builder and maker is God. By faith Sarah herself received strength to conceive seed, and she bore a child when she was past the age, because she judged Him faithful who had promised. Therefore, from one man, and him as good as dead, were born as many as the stars of the sky in multitude—innumerable as the sand which is by the seashore. These all died in faith, not having received the promises, but having seen them afar off were assured of them, embraced them, and confessed that they were strangers and pilgrims on the earth. For those who say such declare plainly that they seek a homeland. And truly if they had called to mind that country from which they had come out, they would have had opportunity to return. But now they desire a better that is a heavenly country. Therefore, God is not ashamed to be called their God, for he has prepared a city for them. By faith Abraham when he was tested, offered up Isaac, and he who had received the promises offered up his only begotten son, of whom it was said, "In Isaac your seed shall be called," accounting that God was able to raise him up, even from the dead, from which he also received him in a figurative sense. By faith Isaac blessed Jacob and Esau concerning things to come. By faith Jacob when he was dying, blessed each of the sons of Joseph and worshipped, leaning on the top of his staff. By faith Joseph when he was dying, made mention of the departure of the children of Israel, and gave instructions concerning his bones. By faith Moses when he was born, was hidden three months by his parents, because they saw he was a beautiful child; and they were not afraid of the king's command. By faith Moses when he became of age, refused to be called the son of Pharaoh's daughter, choosing rather to suffer affliction with the people of God than to enjoy the passing pleasure of sin, esteeming the reproach of Christ greater riches than the treasures of Egypt; for he looked to the reward. By faith he forsook Egypt, not fearing the wrath of the king for he endured as seeing Him who is invisible. By faith he kept the Passover and the sprinkling of blood, lest he who destroyed the firstborn should touch them. By faith he passed through the Red Sea as by dry land, whereas the Egyptians attempting to do so were drowned. By faith the walls of Jericho fell down, after they were encircled for seven days. By faith the harlot Rahab did not perish with those who did not believe, when she had received the spies with peace. And what more shall I say? For the time would fail me to tell of Gideon and Barak and Samson and Jephthah, also of David and Samuel and the prophets: who through faith subdued kingdoms, worked righteousness, obtained promises, stopped the mouths of lions, quenched the violence of fire, escaped the edge of the sword, out of

141

weakness were made strong, became valiant in battle, turned to flight the armies of aliens. Women received their dead back to life again. And others were tortured not accepting deliverance, that they might obtain a better resurrection. Still others had trials of mocking's and scourging's, yes, and of chains and imprisonment. They were stoned, they were sawn in two, were tempted, were slain with the sword. They wandered about in sheepskins and goatskins, being destitute, afflicted, tormented—of whom the world was not worthy. They wandered in dens and caves of the earth. And all these, having obtained a good testimony through faith, did not receive the promise, God having provided something better for us, that they should not be made perfect apart from us. Therefore we also, since we are surrounded by so great a cloud of witnesses, let us lay aside every weight, and the sin which so easily ensnares us, and let us run with endurance the race that is set before us, looking unto Jesus, the author and finisher of our faith, who for the joy that was set before Him endured the cross, despising the shame, and has sat down at the right hand of the throne of God. Hebrews 11: 1-40 and 12:1-2

Reading this portion of scripture is like taking an adventure, a marvelous adventure through time. We see all that have gone before and lived a life of faith. I wanted you to read this entire portion of scripture because this is the hall of faith. These are the heroes of faith. They have paved the way to God for the rest of us. They made the path for us to follow. They blazed a trail through the wilderness of this world and gave us a clearer path and a clearer vision of God and how to serve Him. They did this through their obedience, through their suffering and through their willingness to lay down their lives. Yes, it was through faith.

This is the Great Hall of Faith. These are the great cloud of witnesses. Oh, it is much bigger than those listed here, this is just a sample. To belong here is the greatest honor to ever be bestowed, anywhere, for all eternity in any place, ever. There are honors given on earth, some deserved and some not, but they cannot compare with belonging in this eternal hall of faith. This is the greatest honor. The honors and rewards of earth cannot begin to compare with the honor of a place in the Great Hall of Faith. The medals they wear are their scars from earth, which will be with them for eternity, just as the scars on Jesus hands and feet are still plainly seen. I love to read this passage and walk through here and wave to my heroes, Enoch and Noah, Joseph and Moses and many more. I love this place.

But the Hall of Faith is not finished yet. There are many seats left there to be filled and many are at the front. For the greatest battle of all time is before us. The final call to the Hall of Faith has been sounded. Can you hear it? You have been invited to this glorious place. You have been invited to join these glorious overcomers who belong in the Hall of Faith.

The heroes of faith are lined up and waiting. Now, their attention is on us. Those of us who choose the same path they chose. It is the path of total commitment to God. It is the path that walks through the dark world, shining the Light of Christ. Their attention is on us, and they are waiting for us to run our race with faith and join them. We are told that they can't be made perfect apart from us. They need us as we need them. They love us with a love we cannot understand. They are like grandparents who wanted the best for us, so they did not live for themselves, but for us, the generations that would follow them. There is no competition. They want you to run farther than they did and faster than they did. They are watching and cheering, rooting for you. Your success is their success because it was for you. They have truly become like Christ. They are His followers. They are our family.

You can run this race, as they did. It takes laying aside every weight that would slow you down. It takes running with endurance. It takes keeping your eyes fixed on Jesus, the only One who ran this race perfectly. He is the Author and the finisher of our faith.

We do not have to know the measure of what we accomplish, in our struggles on earth. We have no idea the true value of a life dedicated to God and lived in faith and obedience. It is beyond our limited understanding. Some people's lives may look like complete failures, to others and even to ourselves. We cannot possibly realize the effect a life of faith can have on those around them, or on those who come after them. We don't understand yet what kind of affect we have on the invisible realm, the real world, the eternal world, when we lay down our lives and pick up our crosses.

Those present in Jesus time, those who stood

gazing at a man, suffering on a cross, had no idea of the importance of what they were seeing. Some of them mocked him, some spit on Him, some cried bitter tears. Some of them had hoped he would become their King. It looked to them like a total loss, a waste of a life, a shame.

They did not comprehend what was happening. The single greatest event of all eternity of all time was being played out before their very eyes and no one knew it. All of mankind since Adam was doomed because of sin and no one knew God's answer was this suffering man on a cross. He was the answer to pain and suffering to sickness and death and most importantly to eternal death.

Something was happening in the real world, the spirit world, a world invisible to them. The Light of the world, the Creator of the universe, the Son of God was suffering there before them. Soon He breathed His last breath. The sun grew dark, and the earth shook. Little did they know Jesus had entered into hell and defeated the hosts of darkness and retrieved the keys of death and hell. And then from hell he arose to heaven, the Victor, the filler of all things. But none of this was seen from earth. All they saw was loss.

There are many now in eternity, standing in the hall of faith, who lived their lives in total obscurity. The focus of their life was not to make a name for themselves, or to become important. The focus of their life was to be faithful to God. This is true faith. To obey His voice and do the things He had called you to do on this earth. To obey his statutes and His laws and commandments, to live by the words in the Bible and ignore the message of the world, or even the message your own emotions scream at you. True faith is to refuse to doubt that God is good even when you don't understand what is going on or why.

We see in our text the unbelievable price that some have paid for faith. Some were beaten and stoned, some were sawn in two, and they wandered about in dens and caves of the earth. Their faith did not fail. They have an eternal place in the great Hall of Faith.

You can join these in the Hall of Faith. The invitation has gone out to you. The books of eternity are still being written and your story of faith can join theirs. You don't have to be smart or beautiful or rich. You don't need a college degree. You are not too young or too old. It is not too late. You can start right now. Simply tell God you are ready.

Chapter Twenty

The Focus of Faith

I visited a church one time. They had a special speaker from out of town; he was an overseer of the pastor. This visiting pastor was preaching on faith. It was his version of faith. He was strutting around proud as a peacock telling us how God had given him a Jaguar. Just in case you didn't know a Jaguar is a very high-priced car. The title of his sermon was Blessing the Man of God. He meant himself. We were supposed to give this man who drives a Jaguar more money, so we could be blessed. I have seen a lot of this attitude in the body of Christ. I am sure you have too. Ministers preaching on getting rich, and the way we are supposed to get rich is to send them money, so God can bless us. Some of them live in million-dollar mansions. The focus of their faith is money, and they want us to be the same way. I accepted this teaching for many years. I am not so sure anymore.

Do I think we should be poor? No. Do I think God wants to meet our needs? Yes. Then what is my problem? My problem comes when I am reading my Bible. This philosophy just doesn't match up. It doesn't match up with the people in the Bible and it doesn't match up with what Jesus says and the way He lived His life.

Jesus wasn't building His kingdom here on earth. His focus was on unseen things. Jesus came here for a purpose, God's purpose. He had a destiny to fulfill, and He did not become sidetracked. He came here to build God's kingdom and to defeat the enemy's kingdom. He had the most important purpose of all, to redeem mankind. Jesus constantly used faith and did miracles. But Jesus focus was always on building an eternal kingdom. He did not build any buildings while He was here. He never saved for retirement. He did not take up offerings for Himself. He did not worry about things, like what He would eat or drink or what He would wear or where He would live. His needs were met though. He had the ability through faith to feed five thousand people with a little boy's lunch. When He didn't have a boat, to cross the Sea of Galilee, He walked on the water. When He needed money for taxes it came out of a fish's mouth. His needs were met, but the focus of His faith was on building God's kingdom, not on what He could get for Himself.

What about the Bible's heroes of faith? Were they building themselves a kingdom or were they building God's kingdom? By faith Noah built an ark. What a huge task to build an ark and shelter two of every kind of animal, and his family from a global destruction. Noah did this because it was God's plan, and it was Noah's divine destiny. Noah focused his faith on fulfilling his destiny and purpose in God's plan.

And what about Abraham? He was very rich, but he focused his faith on obedience to God. The Bible tells us that he dwelt in tents in the land God sent him to because he was waiting for a city whose builder and maker was God. Abraham also focused his faith on the unseen and on the eternal. He was so focused on obedience to God he didn't flinch when God told him to sacrifice his only son to Him.

What about Moses, did he use his faith to get riches for himself? No, just the opposite. The Bible tells us, *By faith Moses, when he became of age, refused to be called the son of Pharaoh's daughter, choosing rather to suffer affliction with the people of God than to enjoy the passing pleasures of sin, esteeming the reproach of Christ greater riches than the treasures in Egypt; for he looked to the reward. Hebrews 11:24-26 Moses* was living in wealth and splendor, the grandson of the Pharaoh. Instead, Moses focused his faith in fulfilling his purpose and he turned his back on great wealth. He overcame many obstacles, by faith, to lead the Hebrew slaves out of Egypt. Moses needs were certainly met, in miraculous ways. He walked in great faith at one point leading the people through the Red Sea on dry land! And defeating the entire Egyptian army without a fight!

Are you beginning to see what our faith should be

focused on? It should be focused on fulfilling your part in the plan of God and doing the things He has called you to do. As you obey Him you can expect miracles if need be. You can expect your needs to be met. I am not saying we should not believe God for the things we need or even the things we want. We all need things to live here on this planet. What I am telling you is a life of faith, is a life lived for God. It is a life focused on Jesus.

My natural inclination is to ask God for anything that makes my life easier. I go to great lengths in my asking. I want money, enough to pay off my mortgage, and then some. I want a car that never breaks down, with an air conditioner that works. I would like a better job that pays better. I would like to stay home when it snows and all summer off with pay. Also, I want better jobs for my kids. I want God to supernaturally zap off fifty pounds. I want a vacation in Hawaii {well as long as I am asking, I might as well make it good}. I want my husband, my kids and my grandkids to all be perfect people, serving the Lord with all their hearts and never wavering. Are you beginning to see my problem, or should I say God's problem? Yes, I really pray for all those things and then some. It is all about me, me, me. It is all about my life being easy. It couldn't possibly be God's will for my life to be so hard, could it? If I had more faith then wouldn't my life be perfect, with no problems?

God has a completely different agenda than I do. I want everything to be easy. I don't want to face huge problems. I have a nice comfortable idea what life should be like, and I keep asking God to make it like that. I haven't got all those things yet, but to be honest I still ask for those things, I want them. But that is not faith.

God sees way beyond my life on earth. Yes, He has a plan for my life on earth, but He is also preparing me for an eternal purpose. How I live my life on earth will bear on my eternity. It will bear on where I will spend it, in heaven or in hell. It will also bear on the position I will be in, forever. God has high hopes for us. He wants us to pass the test of life with flying colors. He wants us to grow up and mature and become Christ like. He wants us to achieve a high calling. I have serious work to do, and I have serious changes to make. I cannot sleep away my life in comfort, although it seems nice. God has rocked my boat for my own good. It is His will to bless me, but only in a way that will not harm me or stunt my growth. He does not want me to make my life about security on this earth, this swiftly passing realm.

And there is more. We are only in this plane of existence for a brief period. How we live this life of ours will not only affect our own eternity but also others. We cannot even comprehend the importance of the job we have before us. We cannot be allowed to float down a careless stream of existence, lulled to believe that life is just about being happy in these few years, wearing the same blinders as those who are under the deception of the prince of the power of the air. We are the hands and feet of Christ in this physical plane, this earthly realm.

Satan also uses humans to promote his ghastly kingdom. Why anyone would want to is beyond me. Some rock groups have made pacts with the devil to serve him and in return they become rich and famous. It is a small price to pay for eternity in hell and that is the end result if they don't repent. Satan uses world leaders also, anyone he can. We all saw what he accomplished through Adolph Hitler, who is now in a place he will never be able to hurt anyone again, ever. The devil needs people to affect this world, and so does God.

We have an opportunity now, to fulfill God's divine purpose for our lives and be used by Him. We have an opportunity through faith and obedience to defeat Satan and take spoil for the kingdom of God. And we do this through faith, by doing our part in God's huge plan, and being obedient in every way possible. And remember, it is God's plan; but it takes faith to live it out.

So how do we focus our faith?

Do we focus on worldly wealth and driving Jaguars? Should we live in poverty?

Do we focus our faith on making our life easy?

And when we ask God for something do, we focus our faith on ourselves?

Am I good enough? Do I read my Bible enough, or have I been to church enough?

Do we ask ourselves, "Am I a good Christian?" And then answer ourselves, "Well, no, so God probably won't help me anyway."

No, no, no, remember, our faith is not and never has been about us. It is about God. He is good. He loves us. He is able. And is He willing? Yes, unless He sees a bigger picture and is preparing or maturing us and it is necessary for us to go a different route. He will always do what He

152

thinks best for us, and that is what is really best for us.

So, is He willing to answer or prayers?

Yes, but it is not based on your performance as a Christian, remember your Jesus, blow up sumo wrestler suit. Faith is the giant arm that reaches up and pulls what we need out of the unseen realm.

But there is more to faith than getting what we need from God!

Faith is even deeper than that.

Our faith is to be focused on the Lord Jesus Christ and the cross. Through Jesus we have been redeemed from the kingdom of darkness, we are now light. This is our salvation. Our faith should be focused on staying our course with Him, on faith in His goodness, His ability, and His wisdom to lead us.

You see there is a whole package to faith. It is not just about getting what we need from God in an emergency. "God please get me through this crisis, I need you, from now on I'll serve you, just get me out of this mess!"

Many live like that and think that is what faith is. That is called the hokey pokey. You put your left hand in, you take your left hand out, you put your right foot in, you take your right foot out. We need to put our whole self in and never take it out, and that is what faith is all about.

Make your life about God. That is faith. It affects what you do with your time, how you treat your mate, how you treat your family, how you do your job. It affects what you do when no one is looking. It affects the words that come out of your mouth. Do they please Him? The whole picture is about turning your life over to God to do with what He wants. You go when He says, go, you stay when He says, stay. You obey Him, His voice, His statutes, His laws and His commandments. You follow Him just like Abraham the father of faith, even though you don't even know where you are going. You trust in His ability and not your own.

It means laying your life down if necessary. It means staying where you are being faithful right there because that is where He put you, even though it seems your life is being wasted. It is His to waste. It means being faithful to the responsibilities He has given you because you will answer to Him. How did you treat the wife He gave you, the husband, the children, the parents? Faith takes every opportunity to show love to your family seriously, because they belong to God.

Faith goes farther than that. Faith goes out when God sends you even if the sea is in the way, knowing as you put your foot in the water, the sea will part. Faith knows that God will take the few crumbs of your life and multiply them and feed the thousands with them. Faith will face a giant, build an ark or die on a cross.

The focus of our faith is to be faithful with your life, like Jesus was faithful, to trust God, to follow God and to obey God.

I love the words of Shadrach, Meshach and Abed-Nego in the book of Daniel. King Nebuchadnezzar had built a huge golden statue and then commanded that everyone bow down and worship it. The King was furious when they refused.

He said, *"Now if you are ready at the time you hear the sound of the horn, flute, harp, lyre and psaltery, in symphony, with all kinds of music, and you fall down and worship the image which I have made, good! But if you do not worship, you shall be cast immediately into the midst of a burning fiery furnace. And who is the god who will deliver you from my hands?*

Shadrach Meshach and Abed-Nego answered and said to the king, "O Nebuchadnezzar, we have no need to answer you in this matter. If that is the case our God whom we serve is able to deliver us from your hand, O king. But if not, let it be known to you, O king, that we do not serve your gods, nor we will worship the gold image you have set up." Daniel 3:15-18

I love this. In other words, they told the king, "God can save us, but even if He doesn't, we still won't worship your statue." This was not doubt, when they said, *even if He doesn't*, this was faith. They were going to serve God regardless. Whether they lived or died. This is faith; they were all in no matter what. We all, of course, know the king did throw them in the fiery furnace and God did save them!

We should have this same attitude; I will serve God, no matter what. Even if we don't understand what is going on, even when all seems lost, even if we are facing a fiery furnace.

When I had my third child God told me I needed to have faith, or I would die. I thought I might die because sometimes I had faith and sometimes I didn't. I had received huge miracles from God in the past, but I kept thinking that having enough faith would mean my life would be perfect. It was far from perfect. I wasn't even sure what exactly what faith was. I thought it was a confident feeling, where I had successfully chased every doubt away, and a state of mind of complete confidence.

And how was I going to know if I had enough faith not to die? I didn't want to die, I wanted to raise my children. I asked God to help me to have faith. When I did every single area of my life was shaken and tested. Every single day was a trial. Everything was so out of control that I just totally let go of my life and put it in God's hands. I had no other choice. I found out that was exactly where I needed to be, out of control, completely in God's hands, the safest place to be.

Faith wasn't about me at all. It was about God.

So, what is faith?

In Summer's language: It is putting all your eggs in one basket,

God's basket.

Epilogue

Jesus came to earth in the form of a man, out of incredible love for you. If you were the only person on this earth, He still would have come for you. He has become the answer to your biggest problem. Sin, we are separated from God. We have the same destiny as the devil and are without hope, except..... Jesus has become our Way, He is our hope, our only hope. He has come and laid down His life, for you. He has taken your sins upon Himself and paid the price for them. There is no greater love than this. You will never experience any greater love than this, not from anyone. Would you like to make Jesus your Way today? Pray with me.

Dear Jesus,

Thank you for becoming the Way for me. I need You and I want You. Please come into my heart. Forgive my sins. I give myself to You. Amen

Notes

Chapter 5............*The Final Quest,* by Rick Joyner, Morning Star Publications,
Pineville N.C. pages 63-64

Chapter 10.........*I Believe in Visions*, by Kenneth Hagin,
Spire books

I Saw Heaven, by Roberts Liardon, Roberts Liardon Ministries
Minneapolis, MN page 19

Chapter 11.........*Appointments with Heaven*, by Reggie Anderson, Tyndale Momentum
pages 80, 81, 82

Chapter 14.......*The Call,* by Rick Joyner, Morning Star Publications,
Charlotte, NC pages 60-61

Chapter 15.....*The Final Quest,* by Rick Joyner, Morning Star Publications,
Pineville N.C. pages 142-143

Chapter 16 ......*Like a Mighty Wind*, by Mel Tari, Creation House

www.ingramcontent.com/pod-product-compliance
Lightning Source LLC
LaVergne TN
LVHW011353080426
835511LV00005B/267